The Embattled Triangle

MOSCOW—PEKING—NEW DELHI

The
Embattled Triangle
MOSCOW—PEKING—NEW DELHI

Harish Kapur

Professor in International Relations
The Graduate Institute of International Studies
GENEVA

Humanities Press
NEW YORK 1973

First Published 1973
ABHINAV PUBLICATIONS
E-37 Hauz Khas New Delhi-110016

ISBN 39 — 100301 — 1

PRINTED IN INDIA

Published by S. Malik for Abhinav Publications E-37 Hauz Khas
New Delhi and Printed at India Printers 423 Esplanade Road Delhi-6

Introduction

One of the major events affecting the international system since World War II is the rapid resurgence of the third world. Within a remarkably short period of time, almost the whole of subjugated Africa and Asia had become independent, and many parts of Latin America were clearly seeking a measure of disengagement from their powerful northern neighbour.

That this was an event of staggering dimension is evident from the fact that the majority of nations constituting the international system belong to the third world, and that most of the political convulsions, armed conflicts and revolutionary upheavals are centred in this area.

Evidently these historic permutations could not escape the attention of the major powers who were competing or aspiring to compete for global influence, for the area was too big, the population too large, economic resources too important and political developments too eventful to be ignored or to be permitted to slide under the protective influence of a competing major power.

International relations since World War II are thus marked by a gigantic major power battle to gain influence in the third world. Evidently, certain unwritten rules have to be respected, and some restraints have to be mutually exercised in order to avoid a general holocaust engulfing the entire world; but within this reciprocally acceptable framework and limitations, all efforts were deployed and all means used to make friends and influence countries. Even a cursory glance at the policies of the United States, the Soviet Union and China would clearly show the great lengths to which the three contestants have gone to undermine each other and to advance their own national interests. Consider the unconcern of the two Communist giants at the decimation of the international Communist movement as long as their own interests were advanced. Consider the quantum of military and economic assistance given by them, and consider the policies of all three of them towards the Indo-Pakistan War of December 1971.

Within the general framework of the triangular contest, what is perhaps most striking is the exacerbation of relations between Moscow and Peking. From the phase of great friendship they have moved to a position of intense antagonism. From the original posture of bellicosity against the United States they have shifted to the position of competing with each other to seek an understanding with that nation ; and from a common objective of revolutionizing the third world, they have formulated contradictory strategies for a mammoth battle in the area. Evidently, this exacerbated state of Sino-Soviet relations has deeply influenced the international situation and has affected the policies of many governments in Asia, Africa and Latin America.

In this short and tentative study, an attempt has therefore been made to ascertain how the policies of the two Communist giants have evolved; in what manner they have responded to the rapidly changing situation ; and what are the motivations that seem to determine their policies in the third world.

However, it should be noted that the whole range of these and other issues cannot be exclusively dealt with through the prism of Sino-Soviet relations ; for there is evidently a wide spectrum of other situations and other events which have also had their impact on the perception and the policies of the two Communist nations. There are, for example, myriad domestic compulsions which unavoidably influence the external policies of nations ; and there is a host of other major powers whose policies and whose presence in the area have to be taken into account. Therefore, while dealing with Soviet and Chinese policies towards the third world, an attempt has been made to give an aggregate picture of their policies, establishing—as far as possible—a linkage between the different determinants shaping those policies.

While analysing Soviet and Chinese policies towards the third world, it is evident that one can acquire only an impressionistic view of their behaviours; for the area is too vast, culturally too diverse and politically too complex to permit any detailed generalizations valid for all nations and for all times. It was therefore considered important to examine concretely Mosow's and Peking's attitude towards one particular area or region ; for only by making such an approach is it really possible to obtain a confirmation of some of the general principles that seem to govern their policies towards the third world.

A close examination of Soviet and Chinese policies towards the Indian sub-continent was viewed as an appropriate choice, for it was here in this explosive area that the great contest between the Communist giants was becoming increasingly rampant, and it was in this area that myriad diplomatic, economic and military initiatives were continually taken to isolate and undermine each other.

Acknowledgements

My thanks are due to the editors of *Survey*, and *Mizan*, and to the John Hopkins University Press for permission to use some of the material from essays which previously appeared under their auspices.

It would take me too long to list all the persons who have helped me with advice and criticism, but I must express my gratitude to Professor Jacques Freymond, the Director of the Graduate Institute of International Studies in Geneva for his help and moral encouragement.

Contents

16

PART 1

Chapter 1

The Soviet Union and The Third World

The Historic Framework

FROM the voluminous literature that is now available, it is evident that the Soviet leaders have displayed a continuous doctrinal interest in the developing countries since the Bolshevik Revolution. From an ideology originally relevant to the developed European societies, they have, through the years, transformed Marxism into a revolutionary strategy applicable to countries far removed from the preliminary stage of industrialization. From a theoretical concept aimed at a radical distribution of the already produced wealth, it has been slowly converted into an operational movement aiming at the creation of wealth through the coercive power of the state. And from a doctrine that was to inspire revolutions in Europe, it has gradually evolved into a concept that inextricably linked the consummation of revolutions in Europe with their success in the developing countries.

But, despite the constant manifestation of doctrinal interest in the third world in the immediate aftermath of the revolution, Europe, during the first two years, was none the less the principal preoccupation of Soviet operational diplomacy. It was towards Europe that the Bolshevik leaders first turned in order to encourage Communist revolutions; and it was in this part of the world that they primarily concentrated their offensive-defensive diplomatic actions once it became increasingly evident that revolutions did not seem possible.

This initial concentration on the European continent was dictated by a number of objective factors : in the first place, Communist revolutions in Europe were believed to be around the corner. Many countries in the area were seething with discontent. In the immediate aftermath of World War I, practically everywhere one witnessed the phenomena of upheavals, discontent, economic dislocation etc. And in more than one country—but particularly in Germany—revolutionary organizations were set up, workers organized and strikes launched to bring down what appeared to many to be the crumbling social, political and economic structures.

The Bolshevik leaders therefore considered their own revolution only as a prelude to the rapid explosion of a series of revolutions that would engulf the continent and would eventually culminate in the communization of at least a few countries.

This assessment of the European situation compounded with the general revolutionary mood that was discernible among the Soviet leaders generated a haughty contempt for the traditional conceptions of diplomacy, and encouraged them to take the necessary steps to accelerate the revolutionary process.[1] Trotsky, the first Commissar of Foreign Affairs, made it clear that he had no need for diplomacy,[2] and Lenin, even a few weeks before the October revolution, considered that "the international situation gives us a series of objective grounds for believing that if we come out now, we shall have all proletarian Europe on our side".[3]

Bolshevik Russia's geographic position was the second factor that contributed to the lack of any operational interest in Asia. The region directly under Soviet influence was separated from the Asian countries by wide areas in Central Asia, Trans-Caspia, Trans-Caucasia and Siberia who had either declared their independence from Moscow or were under the control of "White"

1. For details see M. T. Florinsky, *World Revolution and the USSR* (New York : 1933).
2. For details see I. Deutscher, *The Prophet Armed. Trotsky 1879-1921* (London : 1954), p. 327.
3. Cited in E. H. Carr, *The Bolshevik Revolution, 1917-1923*, Vol. 3 (London : 1966), p. 20.

generals.   Thus when the Soviet leaders spoke about Asia, they usually referred to those areas which hitherto constituted a part of the Russian empire rather than countries over which Russia had hardly ever exercised any effective control.   That this was understandable is evident from the fact that the Soviet leaders could hardly pursue a viable foreign policy as long as they were separated from Asia by wide territories controlled by anti-Soviet forces.

Thirdly, the Soviet leaders did not look to Europe only with expectancy and hope.   They also dreaded the undermining of their own revolution through attacks originating from capitalist Europe.   Such a fear was perhaps not unfounded ; for many responsible European leaders had publicly mainfested their displeasure at the developments in Russia, and some had even announced their intention to undermine the revolutionary government before it acquired all the characteristic features of a stable regime.   In fact, an effort to this effect was made during 1918-20 by the Allied powers when troops belonging to some of them landed in different parts of Soviet territory. Evidently this military initiative did not succeed as it was half-hearted and consisted merely of a series of confused and un-coordinated military actions which lacked any centralized planning.   But it was obvious that had the Allied powers really shown determination in their intervention efforts, had they successfully co-ordinated their plans, it would have been possible for them—with their superior power—to undermine the Russian Revolution.

By 1920, however, the general situation in Soviet Russia as well as Europe had undergone a significant permutation, leading to the dilation of Bolshevik interest in Asia.   With the defeat of Kolchak and Denikin, it became possible slowly to bring under Soviet control the eastern borderlands which had declared their independence immediately after the October revolution. Soviet Russia now found herself contiguous to such Asian states as Iran, Turkey, Afghanistan and China; and it was consequently no longer possible for the Bolshevik leaders to take only a theoretical interest in Asia or simply issue appeals to the Asian people to revolt against their internal and external oppressors. Obviously, something more was needed to draw the revolutionary masses of the Asian nations into an alliance with the revolutionary workers and peasants of Soviet Russia.

In addition, the Communist revolutions in Europe, on which so much hope had been placed, had not succeeded. The revolutionary uprising, staged by Communists in Berlin in January 1919, not only failed to ignite an October revolution, but ended in disastrous defeat and physical elimination of Rosa Luxemberg and Karl Liebknecht, the two outstanding leaders of German Communism. The Munich Soviet collapsed after a few weeks, and the Hungarian Soviet Government quickly disintegrated under heavy internal and external pressures. Hope again flickered in the summer of 1920, when the Red Army stood at the gates of Warsaw; but this did not last long because the Poles launched a counter-attack that led to the general withdrawal of the Soviet Army and, along with it, the virtual disappearance of all hope of successful revolutions in Europe.

The Asian continent, on the other hand, was seething with discontent. Almost all the countries were undergoing profound revolutionary changes in the early twenties. Under Amanullah, Afghanistan had become independent. The Turkish nationalist movement, under Kemal Pasha, had transformed itself into a viable government; and the Iranian regime was fast becoming independent of British control. In China, waves of mass protest against Japan had been launched by students. Working-class movements had gained momentum in Shanghai, Hankow and elsewhere. General unrest among workers and peasants in India culminated in a series of large-scale political and economic strikes. And, even more important for revolutionary Russia, the year 1920-21 witnessed the formation of Communist parties in Iran, Indonesia and China.

All these momentous upheavals did not fail to impress the Bolshevik leaders. If Europe had failed them, Asia could revive their flagging spirits. Lenin, who had rapidly grasped the importance of these events, did not hesitate to express his satisfaction over the manner in which Asia was rapidly changing. In almost all his communications and reports, during the first few months of 1920, he pointedly referred to Asia. At the All-Russian Central Executive Committee meeting, held on 2 February 1920, he spoke confidently of the importance of "our

relations with the peoples of the East."[4]   In an interview with
the *New York Evening Journal* on 21 February, he underlined
the awakening of the eastern people "to a new life, a life without exploitation, without landlords, without capitalists, without merchants";[5] and in still another report, delivered to the
All-Russian Congress of Toiling Cossacks on 1 March, he
stressed that in almost every Asian country there was "an
awakening of political consciousness, and the revolutionary
movements grow from day to day".[6]

New strategy for the colonies

Having made this initial shift, the question with which the
Bolshevik leaders were then confronted was what policy should
they formulate, what concrete strategy should they follow in
order to draw the Asian masses into an alliance with the workers
and peasants of Russia ?   A simple declaration that Asia had
become a significant factor was not enough. Obviously a
new policy was needed, and a new strategy and tactics were
required.

It was to these tasks that the Soviet leaders then turned
their attention.   The whole issue was extensively discussed at
the Second Congress of the Comintern in July-August 1920,[7]
and found its characteristic expression at the Baku Congress in
September of the same year[8] and at the first congress of the
Toilers of the Far East in January 1922.[9]

When the national and the colonial question came up for
discussion at the second Comintern congress, it soon became
clear that, although the general theme of the liberation of the

4. V. I. Lenin, *The National Liberation Movement in the East*
   (Moscow : 1957), p. 238.
5. *Ibid.*, p. 240.
6. *Ibid.*, p. 244.
7. For an interesting account of the national-colonial question discussed at the second congress of the Comintern, see M. N. Roy,
   M. N. Roy Memoirs (Bombay : 1964), pp. 368-382.
8. For details see *Pervyi S'ezd Narodnovo Vostoka :   Baku 1-8
   Sentiabria 1920.   Stengraficheski Otchet* (Moscow : 1920).
9. For details see *The First Congress of the Toilers of the Far East
   held in Moscow January 21-February 1, 1922 : Closing session in
   Petrograd February 2, 1922* (Petrograd : 1922).

oppressed people through a world-wide proletariat revolution was acceptable to all, serious differences existed concerning the role of the national bourgeoisie in the national liberation movements and the type of relations Asian Communists should foster with them.

Two sets of theses on the question were presented respectively by Lenin and M. N. Roy, a young Indian revolutionary. Proceeding from the basic assumption "that the precapitalist relations are still dominant" in the colonial countries,[10] Lenin proposed that it was the duty of the Communist parties to assist such revolutions and even enter into alliance with them. But, he insisted, this support and alliance should be temporary and on the condition that "the elements of future proletarian parties, which will be Communist not only in name, are brought together and trained to understand their special tasks, *i.e.* those of the struggle against the bourgeois democratic movements within their own nations".[11] There was an obvious implication in his thesis that the bourgeoisie in the colonial countries was essentially progressive.

M. N. Roy, on the other hand, argued that the bourgeoisie in the dependent areas was essentially reactionary in character, and would not perform the task which had been assigned to it by history. Consequently, the foremost objective was to set up Asian Communist parties which would organize the peasants and workers and lead them on to Communist revolutions. He maintained that the bourgeoisie, even in such relatively advanced colonial countries as India, was not economically and culturally different from the existing social order, and "therefore the nationalist movement was ideologically reactionary in the sense that its triumph would not mean a bourgeois democratic revolution".[12]

There does not seem to be any doubt that Roy's Indian background and his assessment of the Indian independence movement had clearly shaped his concept of the Asian class struggle. An important basis of his distrust of the bourgeoisie, for example, seems to have emerged from his perception of a

---

10 V. I. Lenin, *Collected Works*, Vol. 41 (Moscow : 1969), p. 244.
11 *Ibid.*, Vol. 31 (Moscow : 1966), p. 150.
12 M. N. Roy, *op. cit.*, p. 379.

significant shift in British policies and his realization that the Indian bourgeoisie had favourably responded to the shift. During World War I, Great Britain, unable to keep Indian markets supplied with manufactured goods, reversed her traditional policy of keeping India industrially backward, thus bringing the Indian bourgeoisie into her confidence and presenting the Indian capital with a free field of development. The British Government in 1916 had even gone to the lengths of appointing an Indian Industrial Commission in order to encourage the installation of industries in the country. Consequently, by the end of the war, the Indian capitalist class had achieved such economic security that the government could no longer ignore the demands of political reforms and in due course largely met them by the Montague-Chelmsford reforms.[13] The idea behind this remarkable change, according to Roy, was to split the revolutionary movement by making it clear to the bourgeoisie that it was possible to realise the latter's ambitions under British rule. Although from time to time Roy revised his assessment of the bourgeois relationship with the British and Indian masses, the main theme of his argument, however, did not change.

Both of the theses were extensively discussed at the Commission which had been specially appointed to consider the national and colonial question. According to Roy, Lenin made it clear in the Commission as well as in private meetings with him that the national liberation movements had the significance of bourgeois democratic revolution, that each stage of social revolution being historically determined, the dependent countries must have their bourgeois revolutions before they entered the stage of proletarian revolution.[14] The role of Gandhi, in Roy's view, was the crucial point of difference. Lenin firmly believed that as the inspirer and leader of mass movement, Gandhi was revolutionary, while Roy insisted that a religious and culturalist revivalist like Gandhi was bound to be reactionary

13. The special feature of the Montague-Chelmsford reforms was the devolution of authority to the provinces, thus paving the way for federalism, the introduction of ministerial responsibility in the provinces and the system of dyarchy.

14. M. N. Roy, *op. cit.*, p. 379.

socially, however revolutionary he might appear politically.[15]

Lenin's thesis emerged from the Commission with a number of amendments, the most important of which was the replacing of the words "bourgeois democratic" by "national revolutionary", which undoubtedly applied to bourgeois democratic revolution, but obviously had a more revolutionary sound. While explaining the revised draft to the plenary session, he clearly stated that the aforementioned revision did not really change the nature of original objectives as the task for the national revolutionary movement "can only be a bourgeois democratic revolution".[16]

Finally, after considerable debate, the second Congress sought to resolve the disagreement by approving both the theses. But despite the creation of this impression that a compromise was reached, there does not seem to be any doubt that Lenin's thinking henceforth became the sole basis of Soviet theory and practice on the national and colonial question. Roy's supplementary thesis was quickly forgotten.

Besides the left-wing group led by Roy, there was also a moderate wing in the Comintern as well as in the Soviet Communist Party, which held views different from those of Lenin and Roy. This group was led by Sultan-Galiev. In a series of articles in the *Zhizn Natsionalnostei* in the autumn of 1919, Galiev expressed the view that the Communist leadership had committed a great strategic blunder by placing the main emphasis on revolutionary activity in Europe.[17] The weakest link, according to him, was not the West, but the East, and the failure of Communist revolutions in other countries was primarily due to the inadequacy of Soviet efforts in the eastern world.[18]

15. *Ibid.*
16. V. I. Lenin, "Report of the Commission on the National and Colonial Question—July 26", *Collected Works*, Vol. 31 (Moscow : 1966), p. 241.
17. Sultan-Galiev, who was the editor of *Zhizn Natsionalnostei*, was in the early twenties perhaps the most important Moslem in the Soviet hierarchy; for an interesting account of his life and views, see Alexandre Bennigsen and Chantal Quelquejay, *Les Mouvements Nationaux chez les Musulmans de Russie* (Paris : 1960).
18. *Zhizn Natsionalnostei* (5 October, 12 October and 2 November 1919).

Sultan-Galiev was of the view that the eastern societies, because of their unique social, cultural and religious characteristics, required different revolutionary methods from those used in the West.[19] He therefore put forward the interesting thesis that since the bourgeoisie in the dependent areas was leading the national liberation movements, the Communists should support them and establish lasting ties with them.

This group maintained that "since the national liberation movements in the East are specially led by the merchant bourgeoisie and the progressive clergy, it is necessary that the proletarian communists support all these revolutionary national movements whatever be their form of government and the immediate objectives of these movements".[20] Sultan-Galiev also put forward the thesis that the Moslem people were not divided into rival social classes and that it was therefore important to adapt Marxist theory to the peculiar conditions of the Asian people in general and the Islamic people in particular.

Such views were openly expressed by Ryskulov and Narbuta Bekov, two of Sultan-Galiev's important followers, at the Baku Conference. Ryskulov, who was the delegate from Kazan, stressed the role of the radical bourgeoisie, which, according to him, represented the movement of independence and social revolution. He said :

We cannot expect to have exclusively a communist revolution in the East. It will have national and *petit* bourgeois character but will definitely evolve into a social movement— and since the revolutionary organization of workers is still weak, the *petit* bourgeois democrats will assume the direction.[21]

Besides insisting on the national character of revolutions in the Asian countries which would be led by the bourgeoisie, the followers of Sultan-Galiev underlined the various factors that separated the East from the West and the importance of adapting Communism to the social and cultural framework of the colonial countries. They seemed to suggest that the European

---

19. *Ibid.*
20. Cited by Bennigsen and Quelquejay, *op. cit.*, p. 135.
21. *Ibid.*, p. 136.

Communists did not understand the colonial countries, and it was therefore important that responsibility for leading Communist movements there ought to be assigned to the Asian Communists.[22]

The Comintern delegates to the Baku Congress vehemently rejected Sultan-Galiev's views and reiterated the vital necessity of establishing close collaboration between the workers of the West and the peasants of the East. But instead of countering this argument of the Moslem Communists by underlining the original line formally agreed upon at the second congress of the Comintern, they went beyond it and actually launched the Royist thesis of proletarian revolution in dependent areas. In his opening speech, Zinoviev argued in favour of creating Soviets even "in countries where there are no town workers".[23] Pavlovich expressed the view that all the landlords and the wealthy classes in the dependent areas "were supporting the rule of the foreign capitalists of the international bourgeoisie"[24] and that war in these areas must be waged on two fronts, namely, against foreign capital and against the native bourgeoisie.

The thesis that was finally adopted at the congress thus openly favoured the creation of Soviets in the dependent areas. Clearly this line was in direct contradiction with the thesis adopted at the second congress of the Comintern, and there are some indications that the Soviet leadership did not accept it. According to Roy, Lenin in fact criticized Zinoviev for having "painted nationalism red"[25] and the Soviet newspapers seemed generally to have ignored all that was said in Baku.[26]

There does not seem to be any doubt that Lenin was determined to continue the relatively moderate line formulated at the second congress. Therefore, in the actual formulation of Soviet policy, the Baku congress and all that was said there played an insignificant role. In fact, one can go to the extent of

22. *Ibid.*
23. *Pervyi S'ezd Narodnovo Vostoka : Baku 1-8 Sentiabre 1920, Stengrafi-cheski Otchet* (Petrograd : 1920), pp. 69-72.
24. *Ibid.*, pp. 149-150.
25. M. N. Roy, *op. cit.*, p. 395.
26. Ivor Spector, *The Soviet Union and the Muslim World, 1917-1958* (Seattle : 1959), p. 59.

stating that the congress of the Peoples of the East was nothing but a passing, though undoubtedly important, episode in Soviet history.

The inter-war years

Having reasserted the Leninist thesis, the Soviet leaders were now faced with the delicate and rather difficult task of applying these general theoretical formulations to the concrete reality of the developing countries. But before they could do so, they had to examine the different political forces operating in the area and analyse their objectives and their orientations. Obviously it was a difficult task in view of the fact that most of these countries were at different stages of political struggle and were led by nationalist leaders with different backgrounds and diverse objectives. There was Kemal Pasha in Turkey, Reza Khan in Iran, Amanullah in Afghanistan and Sun Yat-sen in China, who had, in their different manners, raised the flag of nationalistic revolt against the West and who had, at the same time, either set up independent governments of their own or taken over the already existing ones. In short, these Asian leaders were exercising regular governmental functions with the exception that they had not completely consolidated their position in their respective countries, either because of the existence of dilapidated parallel governments or because of the influence of some outside forces.

Also falling into this category of dependent states were Japan and Outer Mongolia. But both of them were different from the other Asian states mentioned above and were, at the same time, also different from each other : economically Japan was as developed as any advanced European country with a sharp and well-defined imperialistic policy of her own, while under-developed Mongolia was unique in that she had, right from the beginning, hinged her fate to Soviet Russia.

Lastly, there was the rest of Asia still colonial and still far removed from the goal of independence. But the nationalist resurgence in these countries was none the less rapidly asserting itself. Everywhere peoples were rising to [rid themselves of imperial domination. In Morocco, Abd-el-krim challenged the Spanish and the French ; in Egypt, Soad Zoghlul Pasha led the nationalists against the British ; and in Syria, there was a serious rebellion to throw off the French mandatory rule. It was perhaps in India that the nationalist movement was becoming most assertive. The rising demands of the Indian nationalists, coming increasingly under Gandhi's spell, went far beyond what the British were prepared to grant, and the Congress widened its base to become a mass movement capable of virtually paralysing the government.

Such was thus the type of Asia that confronted the Soviet leaders when they set their sights on that continent. From the various statements and declarations made by them,[27] it would appear that there was a general consensus of opinion in Moscow that the nationalist governments in Afghanistan, Turkey, China and Iran were revolutionary and, as such, worthy of Soviet support.

With regard to the colonial areas, Soviet policy was relatively straightforward. It was concerned with the basic objective of assisting these countries to become independent. So in effect there were two different types of Soviet policies : one —which could be characterized as diplomatic—was directed towards countries which had already attained their formal political independence ; and the other—revolutionary—applicable to the colonial areas which were still far removed from the goal of national independence.

Towards the independent nations of Asia, the main thrust of Soviet policy during the entire inter-war period was to seek collaboration with nationalist governments and to extend Soviet influence over them by gradual and unobtrusive methods, without of course undermining the opportunities for profitable economic relations with western countries. Military, political and economic assistance was given to the governments of Kemal Ataturk in Turkey, Sun Yat-sen in China, Amanullah in Afghanistan, in order to bring about the decimation of western

27. There is no one consolidated Soviet declaration or article of this period in which it has been clearly stated that these countries are revolutionary and therefore ought to be supported. There are a number of different writings in which views to this effect have been expressed. For details, see V. I. Lenin, *National Liberation Movement in the East* (Moscow : 1957).

influence ; and no stone was left unturned—including military and diplomatic threats—to persuade the Iranian Government to loosen its political and economic ties with Great Britain.

Towards the colonial world, the Soviet policy was frankly revolutionary. Despite many tactical fluctuations, Moscow's basic and permanent objective was to extend open support, both moral and material, to nationalistic forces seeking independence from European control. This policy was unfettered by the confines and trappings of traditional diplomacy, for these countries were not independent states with whom diplomatic relations could be established. There were no national governments with whom the Soviet leadership could establish political or economic relations. There was no question of signing treaties of friendship, alliance or non-aggression with such countries. What the Soviet leaders had to deal with was the rising political forces seeking power to establish governments that would be nationalistic in their objectives, policies and outlooks.

In pursuing such policies in the independent and the colonial areas of Asia, the Soviet Government was often trespassing in Great Britain's sphere of influence, and was thereby coming into conflict with the British. This was nothing new. It had already happened during the time of Tsarist Russia. In fact, the entire history of the last century was, to a considerable degree, a history of Anglo-Russian conflicts. In the Crimean War, in the Russo-Turkish wars of 1822 and 1877, in the war with the Caucasus and, finally, in all the Central Asian campaigns, Russia faced the Britain of Palmerston, Chamberlain and Curzon either as an open or a secret enemy.

When the Bolsheviks came to power, this conflict became even more acute. The British could understand Tsaris tRussia ; for it was a country which, while an enemy, had a social and political outlook relatively approximate to their own and which could be counted on to observe the norms of traditional diplomacy. The Tsarists, in other words, having the same conceptual framework as the British, could negotiate and even bargain. The Bolsheviks were different. Their revolutionary statements were totally incomprehensible to the empire-oriented British. They were in some ways a greater menace to Britain than were their predecessors since they could not be persuaded —at least in the initial stages—into bargaining the future of Asia.

Thus the first thirty years of Bolshevik history also were times of constant and continuous conflict with Great Britain. The Bolsheviks, like the Tsarist Russian leaders, attempted to dethrone Britain from the Straits, to oust her from Iran, to neutralize her influence in Afghanistan and knock at the very doors of India where the situation had become ominous for British interests. But the similarity between the Soviet and Tsarist leaders ends here. The Soviet leaders were driven, by the very nature of their economic and political outlook—at least during most of the inter-war period—to strengthen nationalist governments in independent countries, and to extend moral and material support to nationalist movements in countries aspiring to become independent. The first thirty years of Soviet history, towards the colonial and semi-colonial areas, were thus filled with declarations, proclamations and appeals as well as revolutionary and diplomatic activities directed to attain the complete isolation and eventual defeat of imperialism.

But despite all this support extended to nationalism, Soviet influence did not, however, increase among the Asian nationalist movements ; and imperialism did not really suffer any set-backs. If anything, the colonial powers, during the inter-war period, continued to exercise effective control over areas under their domination.

How can one explain this phenomenon ? Why did the Soviet Union fail to exercise an important influence over nationalist movements when she was perhaps the only major country that openly supported nationalism ?

In the first place, this can be attributed to the fact that during the inter-war years, Soviet Russia, despite her geographical position both as a European and an Asian country, was still a region which did not possess the necessary military and political power to undertake bold actions in areas beyond the heart of Russia ; and the heart of Russia for the Bolsheviks was situated in Europe, for it was in this area that there existed the core of her industrial and military complex.

Secondly, the Soviet failure was probably due to the myriad

fluctuations that were discernible in her policy towards the existing nationalist movements. There were periods when the non-Communist nationalist leaders were denounced for their "reactionary" outlook, and the Communist parties were consi-dered as the only viable and ideologically acceptable forces against imperialism. And there were periods when the Soviet leaders considered the nationalist forces as a progressive factor, and viewed their role as vital in the history of their nations. Such conspicuous and metronomic fluctuations, which were often determined by the needs of Soviet national interests, tended partly to tarnish the Soviet image and encouraged many to question Soviet credibility on the whole issue of nationalism.

Lastly, this blind and often thoughtless subservience of the Asian Communist parties must have contributed significantly to the development of prudence among the nationalist leaders. For, those who were striving for the independence of their nations, the intellectual and often financial dependence on external forces must have encouraged them to discern the non-nationalist character of Asian Communist parties.

The war years

With the commencement of World War II, Soviet interest in colonial areas suffered a serious decline. In fact after Hitler's attack on the USSR in June 1941, it ceased almost entirely. No activity unrelated to war effort was allowed. Soviet scholars including Orientalists became correspondents. The objective of world revolution was abandoned and the Comintern was dissolved. The few articles that appeared in the Soviet press concerning the developing nations, for example, completely ignored the political situation in the area and concentrated attention on the strategic war potential of some of them.[28] In the case of India, one Soviet writer went to the extent of show-ing himself entirely in sympathy with the British position when the latter rejected the demand of independence of Indian nationalists in August 1942. This was not the moment for Indian independence and "the war against Fascist aggression" in

28. V. I. Lenin, "Rol Britanskoi imperii v sovermennoi voine", *Bolshevik*, No. 20 (September 1941), pp. 27-37.

his view required the maximum mobilization of all of India's forces.[29] In fact, so concerned and involved was the Soviet leadership with the important and immediate objective of winning the war, that it was not prepared to rock the boat of Anglo-Soviet friendship by raising the sensitive question of British imperial policy on which Churchill was known to have very strong views. According to Eden at one of the meetings during the Teheran conference, Stalin actually applauded Churchill's eloquent defence of the British trusteeship system, to the visible embarrassment of Roosevelt who was known to be a strong partisan of Indian independence.[30]

The post-war years

However, by 1945 Moscow's interest in the colonial world gradually began to revive. The termination of the war on the European front in May of that year made it possible for Stalin to move his troops to North Korea and Manchuria. While this was in accordance with diplomatic agreements concluded with the United States and China, one cannot escape the reflection that the Soviet military presence in these areas must have brought home to the Russians the revolutionary importance of uncertain and discontented colonies. North Korea had already swung to the Soviet side, Manchuria was infested with Chinese Communist troops and a new government had already been set up in Tabriz, capital of Azerbaijan under Ja'far Pishevari, a veteran Communist and Comintern representative.

None the less, while the importance of Asia was now no longer belittled, the European continent still attracted the prime attention of Soviet leaders. Considering the situation in the area, this was understandable. Almost the whole of Eastern Europe which had come under direct Soviet military control encouraged the leadership in Moscow to concentrate its principal attention in bringing the whole area under its firm political and economic domination. At the same time, the aftermath of war had brought serious economic dislocation and political instability in Western Europe ; and the Communist parties of

29. S. Mel'man, "Polozhenie v Indii", *Mirovoe Khoyziastvo i mirovaia politika*, No. 11-12 (November-December 1942), pp. 46-47.

30. A. Eden, *The Reckoning* (London : 1965), p. 514.

France and Italy had become powerful factors in the political lives of their countries. The development of such a situation did not fail to generate new hopes of kindling revolutionary fires in the heart of Western Europe. But within two to three years after the war, Soviet political and military hold over Eastern Europe was firmly established. Although signs of nationalist pride and independence were still existent, Soviet power over the whole area had indeed become unchallengeable. At the same time the Soviet hope of exercising significant influence in Western Europe was dispelled. Despite the existence of mass Communist parties in France and Italy, Western Europe rapidly asserted its determination to remain non-Communist ; and within a brief period of time the whole area became stable, irrevocably limiting the range of Soviet manoeuvres to minor shifts in orientation in one country or another.

There was obviously a favourable constellation of factors that contributed to the stabilization process. In the first place, the multiple pressures that had slowly led to the communization of Eastern Europe induced a strong current against the withdrawal of United States troops from Western Europe. An imaginative and large financial aid programme amounting to almost thirty billion dollars was undertaken to restore political and economic stability. At the same time, Washington "gave fair warning that, if necessary, it was prepared to meet Soviet force with American force, rather than with mere protests and resolutions in the United Nations".[31] Secondly, the West European decision-makers displayed a remarkable determination to resist Soviet pressures and rapidly reached a consensus that co-ordinated policy and some form of unity of the non-Communist nations was the only guarantee for the effective defence of their own institutions. Thirdly, the radical transformation of military technology—including the initial American monopoly of nuclear weapons—introduced an element of restraint in Soviet militancy and probably encouraged Moscow to abandon any intention it might have had of exercising pressure in Western Europe.

31. Dean Acheson, *Present at the Creation. My Years in the State Department* (London : 1970), p. 194.

The situation in the colonial countries, by contrast, was far from stable. As a result of the stresses and strainsen gendered by the war, almost the entire area was undergoing profound revolutionary changes. The colonial powers, greatly weakened by the turbulence of the war, were no longer in a position to reassert their authority. The Indian nationalist movement's demand for complete independence could no longer be forestalled by victorious but none the less weak Britain. The massive tide of nationalistic revolts in Indonesia, Indo-China and other countries could no longer be contained. And China was deeply riven by an escalating civil war in which the interests of the western world had been seriously compromised.

The Soviet Union could hardly ignore these developments. To have done so would have in effect meant the abdication of the hegemony to the Communist Party of China who, though still far removed from the goal of power, was none the less slowly but steadily moving in that direction.

But this was not all. There were other reasons that led the Soviet leaders to turn to the colonial countries : in the first place the factors that had originally encouraged Soviet interests in Europe had undergone significant evolution after World War II. Communist revolutions in the advanced countries of Europe— originally considered necessary—were no longer considered indispensable for the success of Communism in Europe. A succession of five-year plans had transformed the USSR into an advanced industrialized nation, making it possible for the Soviet leaders to proclaim their entry into the stage of "building Communism", within their national borders. The concept that the attainment of Communism in the Soviet Union required revolutions in advanced European countries had thus gone by the board. Secondly, the Soviet Union had emerged from the war with the undisputed status of a world power, while Britain, France and Germany had been considerably weakened, and had no hope of recovering their pre-war status. Thirdly, the Soviets no longer regarded Europe with the same fear as during the inter-war period. They no longer dreaded an attack from Europe, having effectively brought almost half of Europe under their firm military and political control. At the same time, hopes of communizing Western Europe, either through indigenous revolutions or through military pressure, had been dispelled, and the Soviet Union became a firm advocate of *status quo* in Europe.

The Soviet call for revolution

Obviously, the Soviet Union could no longer assign the colonial countries a secondary role. She could no longer permit the objectives in Europe to determine her policy in the colonies. A new assessment of the area and of Soviet response thereto had thus become necessary.

But the defeat of Japan, combined with the advance of Soviet troops in China, Iran and North Korea, highly coloured the generic Soviet view of the important political changes that were taking place in Asia. The nationlist revolutions, not being of the same dimension as the Communist revolutions, were considered to be formalistic innovations of no major significance, the main purpose of which was subtly to disguise "the continual presence of the colonial powers". The increasing and perhaps unexpected success of the Chinese Communists in the civil war in China was for the Soviet leaders a convincing proof that Communist revolutions were around the corner. In an elaborate article, which appeared in *Bolshevik* in December 1947, Zhukov, principal Soviet spokesman on colonial affairs, sympathetically acknowledged the success of armed struggle in China and Vietnam, and unambiguously castigated the "so-called theory of a third force". He characterized the concept as an "imperialist device", the purpose of which is "to slander the USSR by placing it on the same level with American imperialism".[32]

If Zhukov's article in *Bolshevik* was the first serious and systematic post-war effort to assess the Asian situation, the Southeast Asian Youth Conference held in Calcutta in 1948 was the first convenient occasion to introduce this thinking in the operational strategies of the Asian Communist parties.[33] Notwithstanding the non-controversial nature of the conference, the peaceful transfer of power in some countries was criticised, and armed resistance against the nationalist government as well

32. *Bolshevik* (Moscow : December 1947).
33. For details see Ruth T. McVey, *The Soviet View of Indonesian Revolution* (Cornell University—*Interim Reports* series : mimeographed, 1957).

as the colonial powers was endorsed as the only effective method for introducing viable revolutionary changes in Asia and other developing areas.

The set-back

Responding to this militant line, the Asian Communist parties openly and blindly raised the flag of Communist revolt without making a rational assessment of the political situation in their countries, and without seriously analysing the chances of their success.[34] The net result of all this revolutionary din was simply disastrous ; almost all the Communist parties who had thoughtlessly followed the Soviet call for revolution were isolated from the mainstream of Asian politics. In Indonesia, the Communist party ceased to have any influence in the aftermath of the abortive Madiun revolt of September 1948. In Burma, it was facing serious difficulties and was reduced from a peak of about 8,000 to a few hundred stragglers. In the Philippines, after a brief period of popularity and strength, it was on the run with military power completely broken. And in India, where it had, over the years, established impressive footholds among the workers, peasants and intellectuals, the feckless revolts, organized under the leadership of B. T. Ranadive and later Rajeswar Rao—one centring around the workers and the other around the peasants—plummeted its prestige to an all-time low, sharply declining its membership from an estimated 89,263 to 20,000.[35]

It is evident that the attraction and influence of nationalism was too strong and too deeply rooted among the Asian people to be overthrown by artificially created revolutionary upheavals. And the Communist parties, though sufficiently powerful to create confusion in their respective countries, were not strong enough to take over the reins of power. Even where they had become viable factors, and had successfully acquired a dominant position, it was because they had fervently advocated nationalistic objectives. The Chinese Communists had successfully

34. For details, see Frank N. Trager (editor), *Marxism in South-East Asia* (Stanford : 1959).

35. G. D. Overstreet and M. Windmiller, *Communism in India* (Berkeley : 1959), p. 357.

seized power not so much because of their attractive economic and social objectives, but because of the effective manner in which they tried to meet the national aspirations of the Chinese people during the entire period of Japanese aggression. And Ho Chi-minh's successful defiance of France was primarily due to the projection of a nationalist image rather than to his Communist proclivities. "The strength of Communism wherever it is in practice", aptly pointed out Nehru, "is partly due to its association with the national spirit. Where the two are dissociated, Communism is relatively weak except in so far as it embodies the discontent that exists in under-developed and poverty-stricken countries."[36]

The set-back encountered by Asian Communists was, however, not only due to their failure to project an acceptable nationalist image. It was also because of their reluctance to comprehend the social content of nationalist movements. Many of the Asian leaders, having been impressed at some stage of their political lives by the October revolution, had openly and firmly proclaimed their intention to introduce a much more far-reaching socialist pattern of society in their countries than had been intended by the socialist leaders of the West. Evidently, the framework of Asian socialism—both of the left and right variety—was different from the European movements in so far as the Asians stressed their basic cultural values, generally pursued a policy of non-alignment, and operated in developing societies of teeming millions and low technology. On social and economic problems, though seeking the same goals, they showed greater determination to restructure their tradition-bound societies than the European socialists. Clearly this was in many ways a significant development which merited rational analysis. But the contemptuous and rather hasty identification of it with capitalism not only had demonstrated the extent of Soviet dogmatism, but had also exposed a lack of political sophistication that is vital for the understanding of new trends, new thoughts and new movements.

For the Soviet Union, therefore, this was undoubtedly a serious set-back ; for not only her capacity of exercising impor-

36. Jawaharlal Nehru, *India Today and Tomorrow* (New Delhi : 1960), p. 17.

tant influence over the continent had significantly diminished, but even her image as a great friend of Asian nationalism, so sedulously projected since the Bolshevik revolution, was tarnished. The nationalist leaders, who had in the past favourably looked upon Moscow and had considered Soviet leaders as champions of nationalism, openly manifested their serious disappointment ; some of them did not hesitate to condemn publicly the policies of the Soviet Union. Thus the first time that the Soviet Union had seriously turned towards Asia, she found herself more isolated than ever before ; and instead of obtaining a further diminution of Western influence in Asia, she was now confronted with the serious prospects of its increase and its consolidation.

All these factors thus did not leave much choice for the Soviet leaders. They had to introduce some policy innovations and project a new image of themselves if they wished to exercise any effective influence in areas which were not under their direct control.

A new policy

A rapid change was, therefore, instituted in Soviet ideological thinking and policy. Although evidence of change had begun to appear during the last few months of the Stalinist epoch, real signs, however, became clearly evident after the Bandung Conference in 1955. Instead of striving for immediate control over these areas, Soviet diplomacy now limited its objectives to the task of detaching them from their ties to the "imperialist bloc" and slowly attaching them to the "camp of peace and socialism". The new trend in Soviet policy was, therefore, identified as "working with the national bourgeoisie", and it was more concerned with influencing the orientation of these leaders in world affairs than with encouraging their overthrow by the local Communist parties.

But how could the Soviet leadership influence the orientation of the Asian leaders ? How could it attract them to the socialist world ? What steps could it take to make them less dependent on the West ? The situation in the emerging countries being what it was in the middle fifties, it was obviously not possible to pursue a uniform diplomatic action which would encourage the whole of non-Communist Asia to turn simultaneously to

Moscow ; for the Asian countries were seriously disunited in their international outlooks. Some were non-aligned, whereas the others had sought alignment with the West. In these circumstances, it was decided to adopt a clear-cut attitude of supporting non-aligned nations in their conflicts against the aligned Asian and Western nations. India was supported against Pakistan on Kashmir. Afghanistan was given unconditional support against Pakistan on the Pakhtoon question. The Arab world was encouraged against Israel ; and Indonesia was given complete support against Holland on West Irian.

By jumping into the maelstrom of Asian politics, by supporting the non-aligned nations against the ones that were aligned, by morally and materially assisting those nations who had serious difficulties with the West, Soviet Russia had jettisoned the disdainful manner with which she had viewed the Asian problems in the past.

Such a policy brought fruitful results for Soviet diplomacy. A fund of goodwill rapidly surged up among the Asian nations, who, only a few years earlier, had viewed with great scepticism some of the policies expounded by Moscow. For instance, the Khruschev-Bulganin visit to India in 1955, during which they had categorically supported India on the Kashmir question, furbished the Soviet image in the country. Similarly, the Soviet decision to side with the Arab world against Israel and to extend support to Nasser during the Suez crisis of 1956 was a great breakthrough for the expansion of Soviet influence in the Middle East.[37]

By throwing her diplomatic and political weight on the side of one nation against the other, Moscow perhaps was aggravating international tensions, but this admittedly was an important means of establishing effective footholds in Asia.

But such diplomatic actions, though effective for ameliorating the Soviet image among the non-aligned nations, were not sufficient to make them orient themselves to Moscow. For these nations were inhibited in their goal of achieving real and effective disengagement from the West due to their excessive

37. Ivor Spector, *The Soviet Union and the Muslim World*, *1957-1958* (Seattle : 1959).

economic dependence on the ex-colonial powers. Practically all their aid until the middle fifties came from the West, and almost all their trade was geared to Western markets. Admittedly the non-aligned leaders were aware of the considerable difficulties that such a situation created in the implementation of a viable independent foreign policy, but they could hardly remedy this situation in view of the apparent Soviet aversion to non-alignment in the late forties and early fifties. Thus, notwithstanding the official declarations proclaiming their determination to pursue an independent policy, the options of non-aligned nations in real terms were severely circumscribed. They could hardly consider disengaging themselves from the West in the absence of any meaningful alternatives.

However, after the death of Stalin, and with the inauguration of an overall moderate policy towards the non-aligned countries, the development of economic relations with them became a key lever of Soviet foreign policy. An ideological justification for the new policy was soon found by the introduction of some important innovations in the Soviet approach to the problems of development.

During the Stalinist period, the Soviet leaders did not consider that the decolonization process that had commenced in the aftermath of World War II had brought real independence to the colonial countries, in view of their economic dependence on the West. The transfer of power was characterized as a compromise among the imperialists and the native bourgeoisie and landlords.[38] Through such an arrangement, argued Soviet ideologists, the monopoly capitalists of the metropolitan countries tried to safeguard their economic position with the assistance of the local governing classes ; and the latter defended their interests in co-operation with the imperialists against the workers and peasant movements.[39]

Real political independence was therefore not possible as long as these countries were economically dependent, and this in the Soviet view was unlikely under the existing national leadership which was too closely tied with the West. The only

38. E. Varga, *Osnovnye voprosy ekonomikii i politiki imperializma posle vtoroj mirovmoy voiny* (Moscow . 1953), pp. 330-331.
39. *Ibid.*

way to achieve real independence was through "a struggle of all the working people with the proletariat in the vanguard led by the Communist party".[40]

After the death of Stalin, this assessment, however, underwent a significant change. Though the newly independent countries were still considered dependent on the West and were criticized for facilitating the influx of foreign capital,[41] their economies were no longer considered to be dominated by foreign monopoly capital and the big bourgeoisie. In its place, there had developed, in the Soviet view, the new phenomenon of state capitalism which "has a definite progressive significance".[42]

The new evaluation of the economic and social structure of many of the non-aligned nations was thus brought in line with the new and moderate policy implemented by Stalin's successors. And a reliance on the more subtle instruments of economic and political diplomacy was considered more effective and more appropriate to the new situation.

An unprecedented Soviet offensive was therefore launched with the specific purpose of forging economic links. Important credits were given to these countries, trade was encouraged and technical assistance was offered. For example, Soviet credits to India, the United Arab Republic and Afghanistan constituted 35 per cent. of all investment that was expected for economic development of these countries between 1956 and 1961.[43] Trade between these countries and the Soviet Union had also taken the great leap forward. For example, in 1961 one-third of Egyptian exports and slightly under one-twelfth of Indian exports were geared to socialist countries.[44]

40. *Ibid.*, p. 362.
41. In the case of Soviet criticism of India's economic policy, see Sofia Melman, *Foreign Monopoly Capital in Indian Economy* (New Delhi : 1963).
42. *Nezavisimaja Indija 10 let nezavisimosti 1947-1957 sbornik statej* (Moscow : 1958), p. 32.
43. V. Rymalov, *La collaboration economique de l'URSS avec les pays sous-developpes* (Moscow : 1961).
44. For details concerning U.A.R.'s economic relations with Soviet Russia and other socialist countries, see Baard Richard Stokke, *Soviet and Eastern European Trade and Aid in Africa* (New York : 1967); for India's economic relations with USSR, see *East European Trade Magazine*, No. 22, January, 1965 published in New Delhi.

In contrast to this policy of moderation towards the non-aligned countries, Soviet Russia continued her militant line against those who were aligned. This was apparently done with the firm conviction that the decision-makers of such countries—unlike the non-aligned nations—were holding the reins of power by force ; and that they would inevitably tumble under continuous Soviet pressure. Military threats were thus made to these countries, warnings were given and oppositional elements were encouraged to rise against the existing governments.

But all this was of no avail, for such a policy did not lead any of these countries to forsake their relations with the West. If anything, the Soviet threats only emboldened them to turn more and more towards their Western allies to seek even firmer ties with them than they had before.

The great schism

With the explosion of the Sino-Soviet dispute in the early sixties, the international situation underwent an important change. The international Communist movement, which had managed to maintain—despite Yugoslavia's defection in 1948—a facade of monolithic unity under Moscow's continuous leadership, was seriously disrupted. Communist China violently criticised Soviet policy on problems of international relations, defiantly challenged Moscow's claim to leadership of the international Communist movement, and unhesitatingly declared that the Soviet Union no longer belonged to the anti-imperialist front.[45] Very rapidly, the differences between the two countries escalated into a serious dispute spreading in all directions and on all points. The ferocity with which the two Communist giants are today striving to undermine each other's position is as striking as the ferocity with which they had indulged in indigestible encomiums for each other during the preceding period.

Faced with such an unprecedented situation, the Soviet Union had, once again, to re-examine her overall policy towards the Asian countries. Although the original Soviet objective of seeking a diminution of Western influence in the area continued

45. For details, see *The Polemic on the General Line of the International Communist Movement* (Peking : 1965).

to preoccupy the attention of Soviet diplomacy, it was, however, no longer the only objective. The containment of Chinese Communism was added to it. Obviously this was a difficult task, for the Soviet Union now had to frame a strategy which had to take into account the containment of "right-wing" America and "left-wing" China—a task by no means easy for a country which had hitherto been accustomed to formulating a strategy solely directed against the West.

Soviet diplomacy thus responded to the new situation by forging a new policy which was more varied, more dexterous and more far-reaching than the one that had been launched at the Twentieth Congress of the Soviet Communist Party ; and it appeared to react very effectively to the widely different political situations that Asia was faced with at the time.

First of all, Soviet policy of extending moral and material support to the non-aligned countries was further intensified. Economic and military assistance was considerably increased, cultural exchanges were strengthened, and every political effort was made to bring these countries even closer to Moscow in their diplomatic alignment. The rapidity with which Soviet diplomacy adjusted itself to the rising economic demands of the non-aligned countries is indeed striking—especially when one considers its marked indifference in these matters only a few years earlier. Equally striking was the relatively prompt Soviet acceptance to participate in the construction of big economic projects refused by the West. The assistance to construct the first stage of the Aswan High Dam was accepted by Moscow after the United States administration had decided to withdraw its promise to give 56 million dollars for financing the construction of the project.[46]   Technical and financial assistance was provided for the construction of the Bokaro steel project in India after Washington had reneged from its original promise to finance the construction of this plant in the public sector.[47]

If the intensification of economic assistance was a significant development in Soviet diplomacy, the Soviet decision to extricate herself from an immoderate involvement in many conflicting issues faced by some of the non-aligned countries was even more notable. In the Pakistan-Afghan dispute on the Pakhtoon

46. I. Komzin, *The High Aswan Dam* (Moscow : n.d.).
47. *East European Trade, op. cit.*, p. 43.

question, the Soviet Union ceased to side openly with Afghanistan.[48]   On the Cyprus issue, the previous Soviet position of open and unconditional support to the Cypriot Government against Turkey was slowly abandoned[49] ; and on the Indo-Pakistan dispute on Kashmir, a posture of subtle neutrality was now adopted.[50]   In fact, during the Indo-Pakistan conflict of September 1965 the Soviet leaders went even further. That is to say that, instead of simply limiting their efforts to the improvement of relations with India and Pakistan, they began to display concern over the manner in which the relations between the two countries continued to deteriorate ; and they now began to consider that the advancement of Soviet interest in the sub-continent as well as in Asia was closely linked with the improvement of relations between the two countries. Such an attitude finally led to the opening of an important diplomatic offensive to bring the two countries together to discuss and resolve the issues that divided them. And, as we know, these efforts were successful in getting Ayub Khan and Shastri to meet in Tashkent. The Soviet contribution to the success of the conference was undoubtedly very significant ; in fact it would be no exaggeration to suggest that without the active participation of Kosygin in the discussions, the formal agreement would never have been reached.

Undoubtedly, the changed Soviet attitude on some of the controversial issues is a significant development in Soviet diplomatic practice ; for it was apparently the first time that the Soviet leaders had neither manifested a disdainful neutrality on some of the issues nor had taken sides in favour of one nation against the other.

The adoption of such a policy is not only a striking example of growing sophistication in Soviet diplomatic behaviour, but is, perhaps, also an important sign of Soviet consensus that this is

48. Though it would be difficult to produce an exact text, indicating change in Soviet policy, it is evident that the Soviet leaders extricated themselves from an immoderate involvement on the Pakhtoon question by giving less and less importance to the whole question in Soviet declarations and publications.

49. *Le Monde*, 25-26 December, 1966.

50. Harish Kapur, "The Soviet Union and Indo-Pakistan Relations", *International Studies*, July-October, 1966.

the only effective way, under the existing circumstances, to aggrandize Soviet diplomatic influence.

Perhaps the most significant change—and one that is likely to have a lasting effect on Soviet diplomatic behaviour—is in the realm of Soviet ideological thinking. A decade of post-Stalinist experiences appears to have led the Soviet leadership to adopt a more benevolent attitude towards non-Communist varieties of economic and political development. The vital structural changes in many of the non-aligned countries are no longer contemptuously identified with capitalism, but an increasing effort is now made to study them, to ascertain their impact on developing societies, and to determine the extent to which they are different from capitalistic societies.[51] That these investigations are influenced by Marxist proclivities of the Soviet leaders is quite apparent. But the fact that relatively sober and sophisticated examination of these societies is now eagerly embarked upon is an indication of the extent to which Soviet ideological thinking is changing in some domains. In fact some of the innovations had led the Soviet leadership to suggest that a few Afro-Asian countries, having initially embarked on the "non-capitalist" path of development, were moving towards the more positive and precise goal of "national democracy" ; and that it was now permissible for the Communist parties to co-operate with "revolutionary democrats" under the latter's leadership.[52]

Is it possible that Soviet Marxism might evolve further in the direction of liberal change, responding even more effectively to the realities of the non-aligned world ? Is it possible that the radical structural changes that many Afro-Asian leaders are forcefully introducing in their societies would be, one day, acceptable as socialism to the Soviet leaders ? And is it possible to conceive of Soviet theory evolving to a point where the introduction of socialism is no longer considered as the exclusive responsibility of the Communist parties ? Although the Soviet leadership, at present, hesitates to accept completely the possibility of such a development in Soviet theory, developments of

51. For details, see Rostislav Ulyanovsky, "Some Aspects of the Non-Capitalist Way for Asian and African Countries", *World Marxist Review*, No. 9, 1969.

52. *World Marxist Review*, February, 1963, p. 41.

such a nature should not, however, be excluded, considering the great changes that have already been introduced and the serious discussions that have already begun among the Marxists on the question.[53]

The change in Soviet attitude towards some of the aligned nations, who were either contiguous to Soviet territory or not far from it, was also significant. Despite considerable Soviet pressure in the past, the leaders of these countries had acquired certain political stability, and had shown surprising immunity from revolutionary upheavals. Therefore, instead of thoughtlessly continuing the militant line, a policy of moderation was now pursued. Pressure on Iran, for example, was decreased, the longstanding border problem was resolved, and important economic initiative was taken.[54] Propaganda offensive against Turkey was abandoned, stress was laid on the close relations that had existed between the two countries during the time of Kemal Ataturk, and some support was extended to Istanbul's view on the Cyprus question.[55] Pakistan's disengagement from the West was encouraged, economic relations were developed, and a neutralist attitude was adopted on the Kashmir question.[56] And Japan was tempted by important economic

---

53. See Uri Ra'anan, "Moscow and the Third World", *Problems of Communism*, January-February, 1965.

54. On 16 January, 1966, agreements on economic and technical cooperation were signed, *Soviet News*, 3 March, 1966.

55. During his visit to Turkey in December, 1966, Kosygin stated that any solution of the Cypriot question must "respect the legal rights of the two communities, the Turks and Greeks in Cyprus", *Le Monde*, 25-26 December, 1966.

56. *The Novosty Press Agency* is reported to have released a statement on 12 November, 1965, through the Soviet Embassy in Pakistan, which concluded with the following significant paragraph : "The only thing desired by the Soviet Government is the establishment of stable peace between Pakistan and India, and as far as this basic desire is concerned the Soviet Government equally appeals to the leaders of Pakistan as well as India with the call to display wisdom, restraint and patience. Soviet people are concerned that only under these conditions, not on the battlefield, but at the round table of peaceful negotiations can and should a final and stable agreement be reached between Pakistan and India on the Kashmir question." For complete text, see *Thought*, 27 November, 1965.

contracts.[57]

It is evident that such a policy resulted in the considerable improvement of relations between Moscow and these countries. With all of them important economic agreements were concluded, and with some—Iran and Pakistan—even the question of military assistance was broached.[58]

But it would be an over-simplification to attribute all this exclusively to the expression of moderation in Soviet policy, or to the dexterous manner in which the Soviet leaders had reacted to these countries ; for it is most unlikely that small nations would change their attitude towards the big powers simply because the latter have become more friendly and more flexible to changing circumstances than they had been in the past. Important changes in a country's policy are also due to the fact that the international situation has undergone important changes, necessitating the adoption of new policy. Pakistan had begun to show important signs of disengaging from the West because of the apparent reluctance on the part of the United States and Great Britain to give her unconditional and complete support on the Kashmir question.[59] Admittedly, there is evidence to suggest that the West perhaps was more sympathetic to Pakistan's point of view than that of India's but it would be none the less difficult to produce evidence of complete support of all that Pakistan did to attain her objectives in Kashmir. Turkey too had become disappointed with the Western countries on the question which concerned her directly : the Western posture of neutrality, for example, on the whole

57. In January 1966, when a Japanese Trade delegation was in Moscow, the Soviet Government is reported to have stated that it does not exclude the cooperation of the two countries to exploit the vast resources of Siberia. In fact, *Tass*, the Soviet news agency, published a statement in which it stated that the "participation of Japanese firms in Soviet plans of development would be profitable to both the two countries." See *Le Monde*, 12 March, 1966.

58. Although a military agreement with Pakistan has not been reached, an important military agreement with Iran was concluded in February 1967. See *New York Times*, 20 February, 1967.

59. See Mohammad Ayub Khan, *Friends Not Masters : A Political Autobiography* (London : 1967), pp. 114-185.

dispute between Greece and Turkey on Cyprus, and the United States' decision to withdraw her out-dated intermediate missiles from Turkish territory, were two important factors that led Istanbul to disengage to some extent from the West.[60] Iran had begun to see advantages of being less dependent on the West.[61] And Japan had once again become a major power eager to play an independent role in international affairs.[62]

The Soviet Union, there is no doubt, had made great strides among the non-aligned and, to some extent, the aligned nations of the third world. But this relative success was possible only after she had moderated her policies, and had softened Leninist formulas in order to fit them into the changing realities of the developing countries.

Soviet diplomacy did not thus try to excel Chinese militancy by adopting an even more revolutionary posture ; on the contrary, her diplomatic behaviour was an apparent proof that moderation was considered to be a more effective means of extending Soviet influence, and a more efficacious weapon to contain Communist China and the United States.

But what about areas where limited military conflicts have broken out, or where the "national liberation struggles" against the governments openly allied to the West have been initiated by political forces known for their pro-Soviet proclivities ? Is it possible, in such instances, for the Soviet leaders to adopt policies similar to the ones that have been formulated towards the type of developing countries mentioned above ? Obviously this is not possible, as the pursuit of such a policy would be tantamount to the virtual abdication of Soviet influence in the violently explosive areas, and consequently a brutal exposure of Soviet inability to accept the role of a world power for which she had been so sedulously striving since World War II. Furthermore, the Soviet influence among the revolutionary

60. *The Times*, 26 September, 1967.
61. On 13 September, 1967, the Shah of Iran declared : "I hope the day will come when the world will do without all defence pacts. We shall soon see what is the fate of CENTO". See *New York Times*, 15 September, 1967.
62. See Yoshihiko Seki, "The Foreign Policy of Japan" in Joseph E. Black and Kenneth W. Thompson's *Foreign Policies in a World of Change* (New York : 1963), pp. 517-546.

forces would inevitably diminish, and she would become even more vulnerable to the Chinese Communist charge of indifference towards revolutionary wars. In such cases, therefore, the Soviet leaders are obliged to give a military inflection to their policies—particularly where the Chinese Communists are directly active in their revolutionary endeavours. But the military inflection that has so far been given to Soviet policy has either taken the form of militant verbal declarations or, alternatively, it has manifested itself in the giving of important military aid to Soviet friends. The Soviet leaders, it must be noted, have been careful in avoiding a direct embroilment of their armed forces in such conflicts. During the Korean war, the Soviet Union—though willingly extending material support to Communist China and North Korea—was careful in avoiding a direct embroilment with the United States. And yet, when one examines the history of the period, one is struck by Soviet complicity in the origination of the war. At the time of the Suez crisis in 1956, the Soviet leaders supported Nasser, but publicly threatened to send volunteers to the Middle East, only after the crisis was virtually over.[63] In the Congo, the Soviet Union preferred to operate through the United Nations despite direct appeals from Patrice Lumumba.[64] In Vietnam, which has apparently become an important bone of contention between Peking and Moscow, Soviet embroilment is limited to economic and military assistance. However, it would appear from the numerous declarations emanating from Moscow that the Soviet leaders are determined to go much further than they have permitted themselves in the preceding wars of such a nature.[65] Nevertheless, this appears unlikely, considering the physical distance that separates the two countries, and the serious logistic problem such an intervention would create for the Soviet armed

63. Without underestimating the importance and the effectiveness of Soviet threats during the Suez Crisis of 1956, it is important to note that the Soviet threat to send volunteers was made on 6 November—the day on which Britain and France had agreed to a cease-fire.

64. See "La crise congolaise", *Chronique de Politique Etrangere*, July-November 1960, pp. 696-702.

65. Brezhnev spoke of prospective "volunteers" as early as March 1965. See *Pravda*, 24 March, 1965.

forces. In fact, there is evidence to suggest that even when the Soviet Union, on her own initiative, had created a situation of formal confrontation between herself and the United States, a policy of retreat was invariably adopted once United States determination to resist had become apparent. In an attempt to drive the Western powers out of Berlin in 1948 49, Stalin created the Berlin Blockade, halting all rail, road and river traffic. But in the face of unexpected Western determination to airlift food, fuel and other necessities of life to Berlin, the Soviet leaders gave in and transferred the whole dispute to the council table. Unquestionably, this was one of the greatest tactical defeats suffered by Soviet foreign policy since World War II. Soviet retreat from Cuba in 1962 was even more conspicuous ; for in this case, the Soviet leaders—faced by American determination—rapidly withdrew the missiles they had installed on Cuban territory. This was undoubtedly another very humiliating situation for Moscow. Whatever may have been the reasons that had led the Soviet leaders to stage such a conspicuous and humiliating withdrawal, the fact that such an action was undertaken is an important evidence of Soviet cautiousness in so far as direct military involvement is concerned.

Soviet Russia has thus so far avoided any direct military confrontation with the United States. What will be the future Soviet attitude towards situations that have been discussed above, it is of course difficult to predict with any exactitude. But if the past is any guide to future Soviet actions, one could venture to suggest that circumspection would perhaps continue to govern Soviet military policies.

Conclusions

During the inter-war period, Europe occupied the principal place in Soviet operational diplomacy despite the manifestation of considerable doctrinal interest in Asia. But since World War II—particularly after the death of Stalin—Soviet interest in Asia has continuously increased. Every year since 1953, the world witnessed a growing Soviet involvement in the Asian game of politics. And, today, there is no doubt that the continent of Asia has come to occupy a central place in Soviet diplomacy. Most of the Soviet aid, technical assistance and political endeavours appear to be directed towards that continent ; and most of Soviet speeches and declarations on foreign policy appear to be concerned with Asia and other areas of the third world.

Such an important shift from Europe to the Third World is understandable. In Europe, it is no longer possible for the Soviet Union to make any diplomatic headway, to increase her influence or break some of the diplomatic deadlocks that still continue to haunt Europe. Despite the disengagement of France from the United States, despite the remarkable defreezing of economic and cultural barriers between the two blocs, Europe, politically and militarily, still remains partitioned with no scope for the Soviet Union to advance her political cause on the other side of the barrier.   Furthermore, it is hardly possible for Moscow to attract non-Communist Europe by her economic development and social advancement.   If anything, it is the European countries of the West which are inspiring some of the economic and political changes in the socialist countries.

The Third World, on the other hand, is different.   There, it is still possible for Moscow to make further headway, for the political lines are not sharply drawn, and the countries do not have any reason to consider that they have nothing to learn from the socialist experiment that has been carried out in the Soviet Union.

This manifestation of deep interest in the third world has resulted in the considerable increase of Soviet influence on that continent.   So much so, that one could even say that Soviet influence in the area is as great as that of the United States. Perhaps even more.   But this has been obtained only after the Soviet leaders had finally abandoned all efforts to communize the developing countries, only after they had softened Leninist formulas and had, to some extent, accepted non-Communist varieties of socialist doctrines forcefully expounded by third world leaders.   The third world, in fact, has become such an important factor in Soviet diplomacy that it is deeply influencing Soviet policy towards the West.   Since the unrelenting Chinese criticism of Soviet leadership as insufficiently militant, possibilities of substantive settlements with the West in Europe appear to have diminished. Any dealings with the "imperialists" are immediately exploited by the Chinese as "capitulationism", thereby effectively inhibiting Soviet leadership's desire of seeking a detente with the West.

While the conflict in Southeast Asia has made it difficult for the Soviet Union to take any steps to bring about substantive improvements of relations with the West, they have not, strangely enough, inhibited Moscow from continuing a moderate policy towards the majority of non-Communist countries of the third world. In fact, Soviet relations with these countries continue to develop on an even keel precisely because of Soviet moderation. However, in those areas where conflict exists—such as Vietnam—the Soviet Union has given more militant meaning to her ambiguous doctrine of support for "wars of national liberation", which sanctions Soviet military assistance. Although the Sino-Soviet dispute and the Chinese charge of lack of enthusiasm for local revolutionary developments have led the Soviet Union to intensify her military assistance in Vietnam, Moscow continues to practise restraint so far as its operational policy is concerned. None the less, it must be admitted that the revolutionary upheavals now complicated by Peking's rampageous hostility have brought many risks that the Soviet leaders could not have imagined when they seriously launched themselves on the third world scene after 1953.

Chapter II

China and The Third World

MORE than twenty years of continuously violent struggle, before the revolution of 1949, had made it possible for the Communist leaders to establish deep roots in China. From the vast literature that is now available of the period, it would appear that the actions they took, the solutions they proffered and the strategies they formulated were essentially national in character, responding to the needs and aspirations of China. Even the whole gamut of Marxist thought that entered the country was sinicised in order to fit it to the reality of the country.

But if the Chinese Communists had, through the years, gained considerable experience and cognition of their own country, they were remarkably uninvested with first-hand knowledge of the outside world. This was perhaps natural. For, isolated as they were in the relatively inaccessible caves of Yenan, it was hardly possible for them to keep abreast of the rapidly changing and complicated international situation. Furthermore, their involvement on the national scene was so complete and their efforts for survival so total that it was not possible for them to devote any time to the intricacies of international relations.

Their interest in international affairs thus was indeed marginal ; and most of the declarations that were made on the subject were deeply influenced by the Soviet assessment of the non-Communist world. Regardless of the nature of the issue or the level of Chinese concern, the Communist leaders faithfully followed the Moscow line on almost all the major developments that took place between the two world wars.

Consequently, it is not surprising that when the Chinese Communists, after years of isolation, came into power in 1949, they uncritically accepted the Soviet assessment of the international situation. In fact, even before the complete capture of the entire mainland and the setting-up of the revolutionary government, the Chinese leaders had accepted the Soviet thesis regarding the bipolarization of the world, and made clear their determination to ally themselves "with the Soviet Union, with the People's democracies and with the proletariat and the broad masses of the people in all other countries and form an international united front".[1] For the Chinese Communist leaders there was, on the one side, Soviet Russia—the arch friend of progressive humanity—without whom Communism was unthinkable and with whom an alliance was necessary. On the other side stood capitalist America—the arch enemy—bent on dominating the world, and determined to stand in the way of all the national objectives of China, including her national consolidation by the integration of Taiwan, the security of her frontiers, the projection of her hegemony over Asia, and her drive towards great power status.

With such a clear delineation of friend and foe, the Chinese leaders firmly decided to ally themselves with the Soviet bloc, and to break all ties with the imperialist powers. As a first step in this direction, they signed a number of important agreements with the Soviet Union, while breaking completely with the United States. In fact, they launched a virulent anti-American campaign, and sustained a propaganda effort to denigrate the role of the United States and other western countries in China.

Militant policy

The heady wine of victory combined with ideological militancy obviously did not favour an attitude of moderation. So virulent and unremittingly hostile was China's attitude to all things non-Communist, so strong was her commitment to Marxist ideology, and so new was her experience with the out-

1. Mao Tse-tung, "On the People's Democratic Dictatorship", *Selected Works 1945-1949*, Vol. 5 (New York : 1963), p. 415.

side world, that she found it virtually impossible to evaluate objectively the important process of decolonization that had firmly and irrevocably swept the Asian continent. The Chinese leaders considered it impossible for any colonial country to acquire independence under a non-Communist leadership. In formulating such an assessment, they were obviously guided by the experience of their country which, under the leadership of Chiang Kai-shek, had escalated from one crisis to another, finally culminating in a total state of helplessness and dependence on the outside world.

For any empirical observer of the Chinese scene, such a traumatic experience would have been a convicing proof of the poverty of the Chinese nationalist leadership. For the Chinese Communists, with their long and rigid training in Marxist theory, it was much more : it was the living example of the poverty of all non-Communist leaderships.

Thus, the entire process of decolonization that was in full swing under the non-Communist leadership was considered as nothing but simple formality, not even remotely connected with independence. The peaceful transfer of power in Burma, India, Pakistan and Ceylon was anathema to the Chinese Communist leaders, flying in the face of their ideological convictions. Even the violent revolution in Indonesia was not viewed favourably, simply because the Communist party was not leading it.

The Communist parties of these countries were, therefore, encouraged to raise the flag of revolt against their respective governments. At a meeting of the World Federation of Trade Unions in Peking in 1949, Liu Shao-chi openly suggested to the Asian countries to follow the Chinese path. He declared : "The path taken by the Chinese people in defeating imperialism and its lackeys, and in founding the People's Republic of China is the path that should be taken by the peoples of the various colonial and semi-colonial countries for national independence and people's democracy".[2] Another Chinese spokesman at the conference went even further and frankly stated that the Chinese people would give "moral and material support to the national liberation fighters in Malaya, Burma, Indo-China, Indonesia

2. *New China News Agency* (Peking : 23 November 1949).

and Philippines".[3]   Mao Tse-tung personally sent a cable to the Indian Communists, giving them his full support in their struggle against the Nehru Government, and expressed the view that the day was not far off when India, like China, would be liberated by the Communist party from western imperialism and its lackeys.[4]

Peking thus relied principally on revolutionary policy to bring about radical changes in Asia. But this policy, far from being successful, was in fact a complete failure. Wherever the Asian Communists rose in revolt, they were promptly suppressed. In some countries they were completely put out of action, while in others they suffered significant setbacks.

For China, as well as the Soviet Union, this was a serious setback, for not only had their influence declined over most of Asia, but even their image of a great friend of nationalism, so sedulously projected since the Bolshevik Revolution, was tarnished.

The non-Communist leaders, on the other hand, responding to the groundswell of nationalism, experienced a considerable rise in prestige and popularity. The political influence of nationalist organizations was too strong and too deeply rooted in the country to be overthrown by artificially created revolutionary upheavals. Furthermore, many of the Asian leaders, having been impressed at some stage of their political lives by the Soviet revolution, had proclaimed their intention of attaining a much more far-reaching socialistic pattern of society than the non-Communist leaders of many European countries. Obviously, this was in many ways a unique situation, and a contemptuous identification of it with capitalism had shown not only the magnitude of Chinese dogmatism, but had also exposed the lack of Chinese intellectual sophistication needed to understand new thoughts and new movements.

Perhaps even more striking was the fact that the militant line adopted by Peking and Moscow did not leave much diplomatic leeway for the newly independent countries. How could these nations implement their non-aligned policies, develop

3. *Le Monde* (Paris : 30 November 1949).
4. V. B. Karnik (ed.), *Indian Communist Party Documents, 1930-1956* (Bombay : 1957), p. 48.

meaningful relations with all nations irrespective of political and economic differences, when the Communist countries, highly vitriolic in their attacks on non-alignment, were not prepared to go beyond the simple establishment of diplomatic relations ? For the real success of non-alignment is contingent on the actual acceptance or tolerance of such a line by other nations.

Therefore, notwithstanding the repeatedly announced intentions of the Asian countries to remain non-aligned, many of them, in fact, found themselves drifting in the direction of the United States and the West European nations who, significantly enough, appeared to be more tolerant towards the policies of these countries. Almost the entire economic and military assistance of Burma—faced with Communist and Karen insurrections—emanated from the Commonwealth countries. Most of her treaties and trade agreements were concluded with non-Communist nations. Indonesia, under Hatta and Natsir, was decidedly pro-Western, receiving economic assistance mainly from the Netherlands and the United States. India's relations with the outside world were principally limited to non-Communist nations, and her economic and military assistance emanated from the West.

But, if many of these nations were left with no choice but to turn to the West for economic and military assistance, they none the less adopted an independent line on a number of international issues. In fact, quite often it was in contradiction with the policy proposed by the West. Many of them demandded the admission of Communist China to the United Nations, insisted on the return of Formosa to mainland China, and declined to go to San Francisco to sign the Japanese Peace Treaty on the grounds that Communist China, a major victim of Japanese aggression during World War II, had refused to accept the American draft treaty. A number of non-aligned nations refused to label Communist China as an aggressor in the Korean War, and continued to trade strategic goods with Peking, despite the imposition of a United Nations embargo on such material.

Peaceful co-existence

The failure of Chinese revolutionary policy, and the manifestation of marked political independence by many Asian countries from the West, did not fail to impress Peking, for very soon it became increasingly evident that it was abandoning the militant line.

Although some signs of change had already become evident during the Korean war, the most striking general signal, however, appeared in 1952. At a well-attended meeting of Asian and Pacific peoples in October of that year, the Chinese Communists proclaimed their new line of peaceful co-existence. Instead of enunciating a revolutionary line, they underlined the importance of concluding a peace treaty with Japan, stressed the vital necessity of reaching an agreement between the five big powers, and emphasized the importance of expanding trade.[5] The seven-point message that the conference addressed to the United Nations called, among other things, for steps to end the fighting in Vietnam, Malaya and other countries, and "to bring about just and reasonable settlement through negotiations".[6] The message also underlined the new Chinese view that "countries with different social systems and ways of life can co-exist peacefully".[7]

If the Chinese declarations at the Peking Conference were encouraging straws in the wind, the Chinese role at the Geneva Conference of 1954 was undoubtedly a definite proof of the changes that had taken place in Peking's foreign policy. For it was at that conference that Chou En-lai persuaded the Vietminhs to withdraw their troops from Laos and Cambodia, and to abandon their demand that the governments created by Khmer Issorak and Pathet Lao forces must participate in the conference. According to some reports, it was also the Chinese delegation that persuaded the reluctant Vietminh to accept the unfavourable dividing line along the narrow waist-line at the 17th Parallel.[8] Undoubtedly the Chinese peace offensive, as manifested at the Peking and Geneva conferences, had left a significant impact on the Asian countries. Not only had it

5. *Le Monde*, 5-6 October 1952.
6. *Survey of Mainland Press* (Hongkong : 14-15 October 1952).
7. *Ibid.*
8. Jean Lacouture and Philippe Devilliers, *Indo-Chine*, 1954 (Paris : 1960), pp. 217-218.

contributed to the partial breaking-down of barriers between Peking and non-Communist Asia, but it had considerably helped in the development of the lines of communication between them, which until then were tenuous. It was perhaps this new atmosphere of friendliness and credibility that led the Colombo powers to invite China to participate in the Afro-Asian Conference at Bandung (1955).

If the new diplomacy had left a significant impact on the Asian countries, Chou En-lai's friendly and remarkably moderate attitude at Bandung quelled the lingering suspicions about Chinese intentions. He assured the conference that his desire was to be conciliatory, that the Chinese delegation wanted to "seek common ground".[9] Side-stepping the frontal attacks of the pro-Western delegations who attacked Communist imperialism, he worked patiently to gain confidence, to extend the area of contact with each of the participating states, and to inspire trust in China's peaceful intentions. Even on the intractable issue of Taiwan, the Chinese Prime Minister declared his readiness to enter into bilateral negotiations[10]; and before leaving Bandung, he invited Cambodian and Thai leaders to send representatives to make an on-the-spot check in South China, and thus assure for themselves that there were no preparations to subvert their countries.[11]

In order to meet the issue of subversion, Chou En-lai took the unprecedented step—consistently refused by preceding governments—of signing a treaty of dual nationality with Indonesia which stipulated that the 3 million Chinese residents of that country would be required to decide, within two years, whether they wanted Chinese or Indonesian nationality.[12] At the same time he announced his readiness to conclude similar agreements with other states who were faced with such a

9. The Ministry of Foreign Affairs, *Afro-Asia Speaks from Bandung* (Djakarta : 1954), p. 64.
10. *Ibid.*
11. *Ibid.*
12. For details see G. V. Ambekar and V. D. Divekar (ed.), *Documents on China's Relations with South and Southeast Asia, 1949-1962* (Bombay : 1964), pp. 231-236.

problem and who recognized China.[13]

The remarkably sober performance of Chinese leaders at the multilateral conferences thus greatly contributed in breaking down diplomatic barriers and developing some mutual understanding on a number of international issues with many of the newly independent countries. But in order to gain more appeal and credibility, they engaged themselves in a sustained and massive programme of cultural diplomacy, utilizing information, ideas, persons and culture as a systematic and integral arm of foreign policy. For liberal societies, these activities are basically uncontrolled and generally fall within the purview of independent individuals and organizations. For a Communist nation, they constitute an essential ingredient of diplomacy, whose objective is to project a favourable image, to win friends and neutralize opponents, to gain recognition as an established power, to establish a common identity with the developing countries, and to undercut the western position.

That China was successful in her cultural offensive was evident from the increasing number of visitors who travelled to China. In 1955, there were approximately 4760 visitors from 63 countries. In 1956, there were 5200 from 75 countries.[14] The composition of the delegations varied from year to year, depending on political developments. When the *Panch Sheel* declaration was made by India and China in 1954, the rising curve of Indian visitors reached a high point. When the stirrings in the Middle East took on serious proportions, particularly during the Suez crisis of 1956, the number of Arab visitors increased markedly. And when political explosions became more rampant in Africa and Latin America, the number of visitors from these areas rose steeply.

Thus it became apparent that Peking was seeking to come to terms with the newly independent countries, who were hitherto under a cloud in the Communist world. As a first concrete step in this direction, China systematically proceeded to cultivate those countries of Asia which had opted for a policy of

13. For details about the overseas Chinese see C. P. Fitzgerald, *The Third China* (Vancouver : 1965), *passim.*
14. For details see Herbert Passin, *China's Cultural Diplomacy* (London : 1962), pp. 2-3.

non-alignment. Agreements were signed with some of them, setting forth the so-called "five principles of co-existence", which were to have so much vogue in Asia, and which were subsequently embodied in many treaties and international policy statements made by the Asian countries in the middle fifties.[15] Visits were undertaken to and encouraged from these countries with the specific object of giving verbal assurances of China's peaceful intentions, and every opportunity was seized to encourage them to continue their policy of non-alignment.

But this change was by no means limited to the non-aligned nations of Asia—though they were apparently the principal object of the new Chinese diplomacy. It was indeed a general change englobing the pro-Western nations as well. With Pakistan, friendly relations were cultivated, despite her decision to hinge her fate with the West. Trade was increased, and a large number of cultural delegations were exchanged. The twelve-day visit of the Pakistan Prime Minister, H. S. Suhrawardy, in October 1956 was made an important occasion for giving him a tremendous ovation. The joint communique that was issued at the end of his visit recorded the fact "that there is no real conflict of interests between the two countries".[16]

Despite the apparent unwillingness of Japan to develop formal relations, Peking encouraged Chinese organizations to embark on an important campaign of developing contacts with their counterparts in Japan. An increasing number of invitations were sent to all kinds of Japanese groups for expense-paid tours in China,[17] unofficial trade agreements[18] were concluded, and numerous Japanese prisoners-of-war were repatriated.[19] The Chinese Government even went to the extent of stating that, though rejecting the idea of two Chinas, it did

15. For details about the five principles see Ministry of Information and Broadcasting, *Panchsheel* (New Delhi : 1957), pp. 16-17.

16. K. Sarwar Hasan, *Documents on Foreign Relations of Pakistan : China, India, Pakistan* (Karachi : 1966), p. 363.

17. Shao Chuan Leng, *Japan and Communist China* (Kyoto : 1957), p. 120.

18. For details see Alexander Eckstein, *Communist China's Economic Growth and Trade* (New York : 1966), pp. 210-212.

19. *Le Monde*, 24 March 1953.

not object to Japan's maintaining relations with Taiwan, and did not consider the Japanese Peace Treaty as an obstacle to the conclusion of a peace treaty between China and Japan.[20]

Undeniably, these were major concessions, for by accepting to normalize relations with Japan, who had forged close links with Taiwan, Peking was tacitly accepting the existence of two Chinas. And by stating that the San Francisco treaty was no obstacle to the conclusion of a bilateral Sino-Japanese peace treaty, she was implicitly accepting the validity of the treaty which she had attacked on a number of previous occasions.

The Chinese attitude towards Thailand also underwent a change. Its response to her entry in SEATO was remarkably moderate. During the Bandung Conference, Chou En-lai took the initiative of meeting Prince Wan, the Thai Foreign Minister. He invited him to visit China, and sought to assure him that his country had no aggressive designs on Thailand. The Chinese Prime Minister even went to the extent of stating, which no previous Chinese Government had done, that his government was willing to conclude, on the same lines as Indonesia, a dual nationality treaty concerning the large Chinese majority residing in Thailand, even though diplomatic relations did not exist between the two countries.[21]

Such a policy, however, did not break much ice with the pro-Western countries of Asia. For a wide gamut of reasons, they were overly committed to the West. If, in the case of Thailand, it was an inherent fear of her northern neighbour that led her to hinge her fate with the West, in the case of Pakistan it was the increasing difficulties with India which led her to seek the support of the United States. With regard to Japan, it was the unmitigated dependence on the United States that prevented her from blazing an independent path in international affairs.

The record of Chinese success among the non-aligned countries, however, was phenomenal ; for not long after the

20. Leng, *op. cit.*, p. 92.
21. Russel H. Fifield, *The Diplomacy of Southeast Asia 1945-58* (New York : 1958), p. 264.

adoption of the moderate line, they began to manifest less interest in the West, and appeared eager to institute an equilibrium in their relations with the West and China. One could even venture to suggest that it was perhaps the withdrawal of Chinese pressure that led the non-aligned nations to manifest firm opposition to United States plans of creating military alliances in Asia. Many of them openly denounced Washington for its policy on this issue, and expressed the view that military alliances only served to heighten tension in the area. U Nu stated that the "formation of such organizations increases the chances of war", and made it clear that his government would not be a party to the proposed military alliance.[22] Cambodia declined the unilateral SEATO protection.[23] Indonesia had become so antagonized by SEATO that she proposed the formal creation of a neutralist bloc, professing friendship with China.[24] And Nehru considered that the formation of alliances had only "added to the tensions and fears of the situation".[25]

In the face of this opposition, it was hardly possible for the United States to create a viable military system—Pakistan, the Philippines and Thailand being the only countries of the area which adhered to SEATO.

China's moderate policy was thus remarkably successful; for it not only succeeded in undermining American plans of creating a viable military alliance system, but actually led to the diminution of the feeling of insecurity that pervaded the area in the aftermath of the Communist revolution of 1949. More and more Asian nations were prepared to seek common ground with Peking; and an increasing number of them were now favourably disposed to the idea of developing economic and cultural relations with that country.

22. Cited by William C. Johnstone, *Burma's Foreign Policy* (Cambridge, Mass. : 1963), p. 99.
23. Michael Leifer, *Cambodia, The Search for Security* (London : 1968), pp. 56-77.
24. Fred Greene, *U.S. Policy and the Security of Asia* (New York : 1968), p. 108.
25. Jawaharlal Nehru, *Speeches*, Vol. 3 (New Delhi : 1958), p. 110.

The great leap forward

But such a policy did not last long ; for in the autumn of 1958 a shift in the balance of forces within the Chinese leadership brought tougher revolutionaries to power.

Internally, the "blooming and contending" movement that was launched in May 1957 to generate a free discussion was abruptly ended in 1958. A vigorous programme of political education and Cromwellian conformity was initiated to eradicate doubts and "erroneous" thoughts that were increasingly on the ascendent among Chinese intellectuals. Top positions in higher educational institutions were allotted to party officials to ensure political and ideological conformity, and a number of senior Communists who had shown some sympathy for liberal ideas were dismissed from their posts and expelled from the party.[26] Through an editorial in *Jen min Jih-pao*, the rightist elements were vigorously attacked for conspiring to overthrow the party and the proletariat. "Their threats", underlined the paper, "are a warning to us that the class struggle is still going on and that we must adopt the class struggle point of view and review the present-day phenomena and matters and thus arrive at correct conclusions".[27]

In the economic field, too, the policy of the "great leap forward" was launched with great panache. The carefully planned economic targets, announced at the eighth party congress in 1956, were set aside for more fanciful goals. The five-year targets set for 1962 were now to be accomplished in one year. In place of doubling industrial production, it was to be multiplied six-and-a-half times. Instead of increasing agricultural output by 35 per cent, it was to be augmented two-and-a-half times. Steel output of $5\frac{1}{2}$ million tons was to be doubled in 1958. The country was to surpass Britain as an industrial power in ten years,[28] and Communism was no longer considered as a distant dream, but something which was rapidly becoming a

26. Among those expelled included the Governor of Chekiang Province, the Governor of Chinai Province, the Deputy Governor of Anhwei Province and the Deputy Minister of Supervision.
27. *Jen min Jih-pao*, 8 June, 1957.
28. Niu Chung-Huang, *China will Overtake Britain* (Peking : 1958), *passim*.

reality with the introduction of People's Communes.[29]

Externally, more and more emphasis was laid on the decisive shift in the international balance of power in favour of the socialist countries, on the imperialistic character of United States policies,[30] on the relevance of "uninterrupted revolutions" in the developing countries.[31] But the most striking development in Chinese ideological orientation was perhaps the manifestation of increasing disappointment with the whole phenomenon of nationalist revolutions in the emerging countries. The Chinese leadership seemed to fear that time was not necessarily on the Communist side in the developing areas, and that the new independent governments, established by non-Communist political figures, might stabilize themselves and eventually gravitate back into the Western fold. Writing in the anniversary issue of *Hung chi*, Wang Cheo-Hsiang, a secretary of the Chinese party, voiced impatience with national leaders, warning that they might slide back into the imperialist camp and, in any case, never free themselves from imperialist bondage. He wrote :

> The bourgeoisie which is in power in these countries (Asia and Africa) has played to a certain degree an historically progressive role...It may to a greater or lesser degree go part of the way in opposing imperialism and feudalism. But after all the bourgeoisie is a bourgeoisie. When in power it does not follow resolute revolutionary lines, it oscillates and compromises. Therefore, it is out of the question for these countries to pass to socialism, nor is it possible for them to accomplish in full the tasks of the national democratic revolution. What is more, even the national independence they have achieved will not be secure...There may emerge bureaucratic-capitalism which gangs up with imperialism and feudalism. Thus in the final analysis they cannot escape

29. For details see *People's Communes in China* (Peking : 1953), *passim*.

30. Yu Chao-li, "Chinese People's Great Victory in the Fight against Imperialism", *Peking Review* (Peking : 22 September 1959).

31. Liu Shao-chi, *The Victory of Marxism-Leninism in China* (Peking : 1959), *passim*.

the control and clutches of imperialism.[32]

Apparently, the simple establishment of diplomatic relations and the forging of economic and cultural ties with the existing non-Communist governments were no longer considered sufficient to satisfy the revolutionary zeal of the Chinese leaders. In fact, the continuous development of such links was viewed as an implicit affixation of the Communist stamp of approval on the bourgeois leaders, thereby rendering the goal of Communist revolutions unattainable. Therefore, while maintaining minimum diplomatic relations, the Chinese leadership veered around to the idea of opening collateral revolutionary channels through which it could openly attack the West, seek meaningful relations with the revolutionary forces in the third world, and implicitly expose the conservative nature of the nationalist leaders.

The opportunity for exposing such views presented itself with the establishment of the Afro-Asian People's Solidarity Organization, which held its first conference in Cairo from 28 December to 1 January 1958. For China, whose interest in the third world was evident, this was undoubtedly an important and, in many ways, an historic development which merited more than casual interest. It was the first major unofficial conference of the peoples of Asia and Africa, representing 45 countries, since the Brussels conference of 1927 whose purpose was by no means to voice the views of those who happened to be in power. Many of the organizers were either Communist or alternatively subscribed to left-wing views who had often questioned the process of decolonization that had taken place in some countries in Asia.[33] In fact the organizers of the conference had made it quite clear that the Cairo conference had a character which was "more liberal and more representative of trends and popular interests" than the Bandung conference.[34] It is therefore not surprising that Peking actively participated in the conference and considered it as an excellent

32. *Dix glorieuses annees* (Peking: 1960), pp. 305-306.
33. Nehru was wary about the conference and is reported to have discouraged members of his party from participating in the conference. For details see *Est et Ouest* (Paris: 16-28 February 1958), p. 11.
34. *Ibid.*

opportunity to establish contact with prominent figures who happened to be in Cairo on this occasion. The Chinese role, though not predominant, was none the less important. They were assigned the role of making the principal report on the promotion of cultural exchange between African and Asian nations. The main thrust of the revolt was on the "vitality of Eastern civilization" and the considerable harm that was inflicted on it by the encroachment of colonialism. Warning against the danger of "imperialistic cultural invasion", the Chinese delegate said : "We must be on guard against such invasion so that the vigorous younger generation will not be misled, spoiled and drugged by the corrupting and poisonous influence of imperialist culture".[35]

That China was able to exercise—at least during the first two or three years—weighty influence on the organization is evident from the records of the different meetings. That she attached considerable importance to the organization is clear from the efforts that were deployed to make it into a viable movement embracing the whole of Asia and Africa.[36]

While China's interest in the solidarity movement and its permanent organization was thus rising, her faith in the policy of peaceful coexistence was fast diminishing. While, on the one hand, she increasingly participated in the militant activities of the solidarity organization, she manifested, on the other, an unfriendly attitude towards practically all nations; and by 1959, it seemed as if Peking was at loggerheads with the entire world.

First of all, a carefully prepared campaign was unleashed against the United States, whose intervention in Taiwan Straits and the Middle East was denounced in strong terms. On 17 July 1958, half a million people were brought out into the streets of Peking to demonstrate against United States military intervention in Lebanon. And on 28 August, massive bombardment of Quemoy was begun as a probing operation, presumably

35. For details see *Afro-Asian People's Solidarity Conference* (Moscow: 1958), *passim*. See also *Le Monde*, 27, 28 December 1957 and 3 January 1958.

36. Permanent Secretariat, *Afro-Asian Solidarity Movement. Principles, Structure. Friendly Organizations* (Cairo : 1962), pp. 70-71.

designed to test the strength of the nationalists on the island, and the will of the United States to aid them. Mao Tse-tung personally delivered a caustic assault. In a speech before the Supreme State Conference on 8 September, he attacked the United States' presence in Taiwan and Lebanon, and called attention to hundreds of United States bases around the socialist countries, comparing them to "nooses tied around the neck of US imperialism".[37]

The pro-Western countries of Asia were also made important targets of Peking's vitriolic attacks. In the case of some of them harassing tactics were, in fact, resorted to. With Japan all relations were broken. The two unofficial agreements— iron and steel accord and the trade pact concluded in the beginning of the year, and which provided for exchanges totalling more than China's trade with any other non-Communist country—were abruptly cancelled. And open appeals were made to the Japanese people to reject the Kishi Government in the forthcoming elections. The Chinese leaders now insisted that trade between the two countries was not possible as long as Japan did not nullify the recognition of Taiwan, and establish diplomatic relations with Peking.[38] In Laos, the Pathet Lao was emboldened, in the summer of 1958, to begin an armed insurrection against the existing government.[39] And in Pakistan, the new government, set up after the military *coup d'etat* in October 1958, was denounced for playing "a vicious role in Asia".[40]

Peking's attitude towards the non-aligned countries also began to harden. The first country to be condemned was Egypt. Nasser was criticised for having embarked on a policy of persecution of Communists, and for having manifested serious reservations towards the Kassem regime in Iraq, which had shown signs of pro-Communist orientation. He was also accused of having abandoned the struggle against imperialism, and was warned that people may have to "form a new judge-

37. *Peking Review*, 27 September 1958.
38. *Jen min Jih-pao* (Peking : 16 May 1958).
39. For details see Arthur J. Dommen, *Conflict in Laos. The Politics of Neutralization* (London : 1964).
40. *Peking Review*, 28 July 1959.

ment of them in the light of the new facts".[41] Khaled Bagdash, the Syrian Communist, who was in Peking in 1959, was permitted publicly to characterize Nasser's government as terroristic and dictatorial.[42] And according to Egyptian sources, the United Arab Republic Embassy in Peking was placed under close watch by the Chinese authorities.[43]

Indonesia was bitterly attacked for limiting the economic power of overseas Chinese in many parts of the country, and was publicly warned that Peking would not "simply look on while their compatriots are being subjected to unjustified discrimination and persecution abroad."[44]

India too was made a target of Chinese hostility. The Nehru Government was accused of fomenting the Tibetan revolt of March 1959 and, for the first time, the entire boundary alignment between India and China was formally questioned. In September of the same year, the dispute was escalated still further with the assertion of the claim on 50,000 square miles of what the Indians considered to be part of India.[45]

With Burma, too, considerable difficulties were raised on the exact alignment of the border between the two countries. The package deal proposed by Chou En-lai in 1956,[46] and accepted by the Burmese, was reneged in the summer of 1957 and new demands were put forward. All the efforts of the Burmese Government, which was prepared to go to any lengths in 1958-59 within the new set of Chinese terms to settle the differences, were rebuffed.[47]

It would none the less be incorrect to conclude from all this that Peking had artificially created non-existing problems. For difficulties and problems had in fact existed with almost all the nations mentioned before. The border problems were not new; the overseas Chinese problem had apparently been

41. *Ibid.*
42. *The China Quarterly* (London : January-March 1960).
43. *Al Ahram* (Cairo : 3 October 1959).
44. *Peking Review* : 13 December 1959.
45. For details see Foreign Languages Press, *Documents on the Sino-Indian Boundary Question* (Peking : 1960), *passim.*
46. For details see Frank N. Trager, *Burma. From Kingdom to Republic* (London : 1966), pp. 244-246.
47. *Ibid.*

aggravated by Djakarta's unilateral decision to limit their economic power. In Laos, a new right-wing government had forcibly installed itself. In Pakistan, United States military bases had been installed, and the Japanese Government had declined to give diplomatic immunity to Chinese trade missions under the fourth trade agreement. All these problems had thus existed; but all of them—until then—had been waived. In 1958-59 they were brought out in the open.

What were the reasons that led the Chinese leadership to adopt such a policy? Why did they suddenly abandon the slow but none the less solid process of economic development conceived by the economists, and replace it by fanciful projects formulated by ideologues? And why did they set aside the apparently successful policy of peaceful coexistence for militancy in foreign relations? Was this swing of the pendulum to the left due to the resurgence of left-wing forces in China,[48] or was it really "a synthetic solution worked out collectively after prolonged argument within the party?"[49]

Whatever may have been China's motives for creating new tensions, one thing was certain : Peking had overreached itself. Its diplomatic isolation from the Asian states had become quite apparent, and all the sympathy and goodwill that it had acquired after so much effort had been cast to the wind.

Sino-Soviet dispute

Just as this was happening, just as China was creating tension with the United States and many Asian countries, differences also began to arise with Moscow. At first they appeared to be insignificant. But it soon became apparent that they were serious and covered myriad issues, relating to Marxist theory and practice, and to the nature of strategy and tactics that were appropriate to the existing international situation.

Without delving into the details of the dispute—for much has already been written—it would be useful to dwell briefly on the different views held by Moscow and Peking on the question

48. Donald Zagoria puts forward this point of view in his book, *Sino-Soviet Conflict, 1956-1961* (New York : 1966), pp. 66-74.
49. See Edgar Snow, *The Other Side of the River* (London : 1963), p. 426.

of Asia, since they had an important bearing on Chinese policy towards the third world countries.

The post-Stalinist leadership argued that the possession of nuclear weapons by Washington and Moscow had made war unacceptable. An explosion of conflict, in which the major powers were directly involved, would no longer lead to the advancement of Communism, but to the destruction of all social systems. Therefore, the only rational means available for the attainment of the Communist goal of world revolution was through peaceful but competitive coexistence. This new form of struggle, in the Soviet view, could be successful by demonstrating to the world that the socialist model of development and distribution could meet the material and spiritual needs of humanity far more effectively than the capitalist system. And the only way this could be convincingly done would be through the continuous development of socialist economies, until the entire bloc was to become the most powerful factor in the world, at which point the ultimate offensive against the capitalist West could be effectively launched.

That the Communist world would economically surpass the capitalist countries, that it could eventually cause the continual "multiplication of benefits" for its citizens, of all this the Soviet leaders were convinced. They were convinced of all this, because the stimuli of economic growth of a socialist society, according to them, were built into the social structure. The role of the third world in the Soviet framework could thus only be secondary, in view of their economic backwardness ; for it stands to reason that premature Communist revolutions in these countries would only jeopardize the Soviet objective of becoming more powerful than the capitalist world, since the Communist bloc countries would have to provide massive assistance, instead of concentrating on the task of developing their economies. Therefore, the Communist objective in the third world countries should be, in the Soviet view, to encourage them to develop their "non-capitalist" economies under the leadership of the national bourgeoisie, and the economic power of the Communist bloc should be used for the limited purpose of keeping these countries disengaged from the West. In short, what the Soviet Union was suggesting was a holding operation in the third world, while the battle for world revolution was conducted by the Communist countries.

The Chinese Communists rejected these arguments. That the Communist countries should concentrate on the rapid development of their economies, that they should strive to improve the standard of living of their citizens was an understandable objective which obviously merited considerable and sympathetic attention from all Communist governments. But to identify all this with the primordial objective of world revolution was the height of chauvinism which had no place in the international Communist movement. And, further, to suggest that the economic advancement of the Communist world would automatically lead to the rallying of the rest of the world around the Communist flag, they considered was patently absurd as there was no historical evidence to suggest that such an evolution had ever taken place in the past. If anything, history was full of myriad examples pointing in the opposite direction—the direction of violent change. Furthermore, even if such a line of argument was accepted, what guarantee was there that the "capitalist-imperialist" forces, though a small minority, would not throw a spanner in the unfolding of such a process of evolution in the direction of Communism?

Accordingly, these forces must be defeated by a continuous offensive in areas where they were most vulnerable. And, in the Chinese view, the areas where they were most vulnerable was the third world, which was in the midst of revolutionary upheavals and where the faithful application of Chinese strategy would undoubtedly lead to the defeat of the western world.

Undoubtedly, the differences between Moscow and Peking were serious. And by the early sixties, it became apparent that they were escalating into a dispute, spreading in all directions, and on all points with no hope of any reconciliation.

All this placed China in the most unenviable situation, for she was now isolated from everyone, including her allies and friends. The development of such a situation would be considered as serious for any major power. For developing China, it was disastrous, since she had neither the military power nor the economic strength to completely stand on her feet—an essential precondition for any nation that wishes to pursue an independent and defiant policy.

Consequently, it became imperative for China to re-examine her policy in the light of this difficult situation. So far as the internal situation was concerned, the bewildered government took courageous and energetic measures to meet the difficult situation. A period of recovery and readjustment was inaugurated which marked a change in economic priorities and in the style of economic management. Priority was placed on the restoration of food production, on the formulation of simplified economic planning and on the control of the rapidly expanding population. The People's Communes, for example, were dissolved in effect though not in name, and agriculture was returned to what amounted to the old collective farm. The peasant was allowed to cultivate his garden plot again and raise his few chickens or a pig or two.

Perhaps the most vital Chinese response to the degenerating internal situation was the decision to wrap itself in the flag of patriotism and "self-reliance". When the Russians suddenly withdrew their experts in the summer of 1960, causing considerable chaos in the country, an increasing stress was laid on the vital importance of becoming economically independent and of relying principally on the genius of the Chinese nation to develop economically and militarily.

Externally, however, what could China do to make the situation less unfavourable ? To whom could she turn in order to break the high wall of isolation, without of course sacrificing some of the basic principles ?

An understanding with the United States was considered impossible. In the first place, she was an "imperialistic" nation which had manifested determination to weaken if not to destroy Communist China. Secondly, she had discouraged mainland China from taking any military initiative to seize Taiwan by interposing her naval power in the Straits of the area. Thirdly, Washington had taken upon itself the responsibility of containing the expansion of China in the area where the latter had traditionally exercised influence.

An understanding with Moscow was also considered impossible, in view of the serious escalation of the Sino-Soviet dispute, involving fundamental policies on which a retreat and concessions seemed out of the question. In the first place, some of the fundamental tenets of Marxist theory had been substantially and unilaterally altered by the post-Stalinist leadership. For example, war was no longer considered as an instrument of social change, peaceful transition to socialism was considered possible, and the state in a socialist society was no more viewed as an institution representing the interest of the working class, but that of the entire people. Even the possibility of achieving socialism under non-Communist leadership was subtly—though hesitatingly—evoked.[50]

Although these changes responded to the evolved conditions of post-Stalinist Europe, the Soviet leadership, as usual, was affixing the stamp of universal validity over them. For the Chinese Communists, this was an unacceptable proposal, since their acceptance would virtually mean that their actions were in contradiction with the current Marxist thinking. The important theoretical innovations introduced by the Soviet leaders were leading them to the important conclusion that an over-all understanding with the United States had become necessary. To the Chinese Communists, such a conclusion was dangerous, as they still had major problems with the United States ; and any understanding between Moscow and Washington would render their task even more difficult. Thirdly, any acceptance of these changes by the developing countries would virtually deprive Peking of the leadership of the non-European Communist parties for which it had been striving since 1949.

Therefore, ideological changes unilaterally introduced by the Soviet leaders and forcefully presented to the Communist world had to be forestalled, for in the absence of such an effort, argued the Chinese Communists, the whole international Communist movement would become hopelessly and irrevocably encrusted with revisionist ideas, making it thus virtually impossible for them to exercise any effective influence.

---

50. For details see O. V. Kuusinen *et al.*, *Fundamentals of Marxism-Leninism* (Moscow : 1963).

Consequently declarations were made and contacts establish-ed with the Communist parties in order to explain the Chinese point of view. Every effort was made—though subtly in the beginning—to show the extent to which the Soviet leaders had radically deviated from the original principles of Marxist thought. But all this did not lead to the generation of support from their counterparts in Europe. The revised Soviet outlook naturally responded more effectively to the evolved European situation. The Khruschevian thesis on greater liberalization of Communist regimes in Europe, on different roads to socialism, on peaceful coexistence, on the imperative necessity of raising the standard of living of socialist societies was far more in line with the aspirations of the European Communists than was the rather belligerent line expounded by the Chinese. Therefore, while gratefully accepting the significant role that Chinese defiance had effectively played in generating the polycentric situation, they declined to follow the Chinese path.

Albania, however, was the only Communist country in Europe which defied Moscow and sought closer rapprochement with Peking. But even in this case the reasons can be pinpointed to the peculiar situation in the region. The Albanian leaders feared that their country would be turned over by Khruschev to their hated and feared Yugoslav neighbour with whom the Soviet Government was seeking rapid rapprochement.

When all this became apparent, Europe for the Chinese Communists became relatively unimportant where only limited diplomatic moves could be made against the Soviet Union ; and the third world with its economic poverty and political instability became the prime target of Chinese revolutionary diplomacy.

China turns to the third world

In contrast to her rigid ideological attitude towards the Soviet Union, in regard to whom practically all the orthodox ideas of Marxist theory were reasserted, China projected an image of herself in the third world which was just the opposite. She appeared to stress those factors which were approximate to these countries and which, in many ways, were non-Marxist. The factor of colour was stressed, the issue of European domi-nation was underlined, and the subject of national liberation became a constant theme.

Perhaps the most significant response to the new situation was the formulation of a new theory which partially broke away from some of the basic tenets of Marxism-Leninism. Instead of reiterating the cosmic aspects of Marxism, of stressing the integral unity of western working class struggles with the national liberation movements as conceived by Lenin, the Chinese Communists projected a zonal picture of the world in which the national liberation movements figured as the main force of the world socialist revolution. A Chinese letter addressed to the Communist party of the Soviet Union stressed :

> The various types of contradictions in the contemporary world are concentrated in the vast areas of Asia, Africa and Latin America ; these are the most vulnerable areas under imperialist rule and the storm centres of world revolution dealing direct blows at imperialism...In a sense therefore the whole cause of the international proletarian revolution hinges on the outcome of revolutionary struggles of the people of these areas who constitute the overwhelming majority of the world's population. Therefore, the anti-imperialist struggle of the peoples of Asia, Africa and Latin America is definitely not merely a matter of regional significance but one of over-all importance for the whole cause of proletarian world revolution.[51]

Proceeding from these basic propositions, the Chinese theorists rejected the idea of the hegemony of the proletariat in the world revolutionary movement and labelled such a concept as "the crudest distortion and revision of Leninist ideas."[52]

By 1965, the geographical three-continent theory of the revolution, separating Europe and the Soviet Union from the main area of world revolution, was carried forward into a theory of the battle between the "rural areas" of the world and the "cities of the world". Stressing this point, Lin Piao wrote :

> Taking the entire globe, if North America and Western Europe can be called the cities of the world, then Asia, Africa and Latin America constitute the rural areas of the world.

---

51. *The Polemic on the General Line of the International Communist Movement* (Peking : 1965), p. 13.
52. *Ibid.*

Since World War II, the proletarian revolutionary movement has for various reasons been temporarily held back in North American and West European capitalist countries, while the people's revolutionary movement in Asia, Africa and Latin America has been growing vigorously. In a sense, the contemporary world revolution also presents a picture of the encirclement of the cities by the rural areas. In the final analysis, the whole cause of world revolution hinges on the revolutionary struggles of the Asian, African and Latin American peoples who make up the overwhelming majority of the world's population. The socialist countries should regard it as their internationalist duty to support the people's revolutionary struggles in Asia, Africa and Latin America.[53] Thus the working class movements in developed countries, so far from constituting the vanguard of world socialist revolution, were reduced to an auxiliary position. Implicit in this theory is the argument that the economic gap separating the developed countries from the developing ones was widening, that the rich countries were becoming richer and the poor poorer, that the exploitation of poverty-stricken nations was becoming more intense and that all this will finally cause an explosion which will culminate in the defeat of the rich nations. Thus it became increasingly evident that theoretical formulations and strategic objectives were encouraging China to turn her sights on the third world.

But what could she do to implement such thinking ? How did she orient her policies to attain these strategic objectives ? And what type of diplomatic goals did she establish to create a viable dent on the third world countries ? Like the Soviet Union, China's operational diplomacy was a mixture of a number of different facets. As a nation entrenched with revolutionary ideas, she was eager to build the third world after her image ; at the same time as a state among other states she could not possibly ignore the important but intractable problem of national security. Both the goals were considered important ; and in order to attain both of them successfully a dual policy was formulated. While the one policy was designed to obtain effective hold over the Communist parties, the other was aimed at the emerging non-

53. Lin Piao, *Long Live the Victory of People's War* (Peking : 1965), p. 49.

Communist nations.

The Chinese objective of gaining influence over the Communist parties of the third world countries was natural and understandable. For if China really wanted to see the emerging societies restructured after her own image, it was evident that she would have to seek common ground with those political forces who had similar objectives. Contacts were therefore made with many of the parties, and myriad articles appeared in the Chinese press explaining the validity of the Chinese revolutionary path.

The Chinese efforts, one could venture to suggest, were not wholly unsuccessful. Although many of the parties, in the aftermath of the Sino-Soviet dispute, attempted to adopt an independent attitude and searched for firm grass roots in their own countries, they were not unsympathetic to the Chinese point of view. In Asia, the majority of the Communist parties favourably accepted the Chinese approach, though there were some of them who were widely split. In Latin America, however, notwithstanding the relative relevance of Chinese strategy to the conditions in the area, the bulk of the Communist parties, who were known for their traditional sympathy for Moscow, did not accept the Chinese point of view. Therefore, when the Sino-Soviet dispute bubbled to the surface in the early sixties, most of them underlined their solidarity with Soviet thinking and stressed their opposition to ideas emanating from Peking. However, the Castroites, who have surged up in many Latin American countries, have more in common with China than the Soviet Union. The circumstances which led to the Chinese revolution, the hyper-voluntarist approach to situations and the importance of Chinese revolutionary strategy centred around the peasants, appeared to be more relevant to Latin America than the whole basis of Soviet approach and thinking.

The three Communist states of Asia—Outer Mongolia, North Korea and North Vietnam—also became important targets of Chinese diplomacy. Many of the important diplomatic moves that were initially made and the myriad articles that appeard in the Chinese press were directed towards them with the specific object of bringing them within the Chinese orbit.

In the first place, China probably considered them easy targets in view of the fact that the Communist parties were already in power, and that the Chinese model of economic and political development was more relevant to these nations than the Asian nations who were dominated by the nationalist parties. Secondly, the influence over the three Communist states, situated as they were on the periphery of China, was considered to be of prime importance in order to pursue an effective policy in other parts of Asia. Thirdly, the expansion of Chinese influence among them would in all probability make the Chinese task of exercising influence over the non-ruling Communist parties far easier, as they would, in this case, be able to show to them that the Soviet model was not acceptable to those Communists who were in power, and by the same token could not be relevant to the others who subscribed to similar ideology. For how could the Soviet Union project her own model when the Asian Communist parties, who had already seized power, were not prepared to follow the Soviet action.

With the exception of Outer Mongolia, over whom Soviet hold was very strong, the Chinese efforts were relatively successful. With North Korea close ties were developed following the explosion of the Sino-Soviet dispute in 1960. Close identity was reached on ideological and foreign policy issues. A long-term loan of 420 million roubles was given in October 1960 for the period 1961-64, and a treaty of friendship, co-operation and mutual assistance was signed during the same year.[54] With North Vietnam too close ties were forged in the early sixties. The first sign of pro-Chinese orientation was signalled when Le Duan, Secretary-General of the Lao Dong (North Vietnamese Communist Party), delivered a speech on 14 March 1963. Many of the ideas proclaimed in this speech were strikingly close to the Chinese thesis, and were reported in full by the *People's Daily* and were subsequently disseminated by Peking's Foreign Languages Publishing House.

Perhaps the most important diplomatic offensive that was launched by Peking, however, was directed at the non-aligned countries with whom many of the seemingly intractable disputes were promptly resolved.

54. *Peking Review*, 18 October 1960.

Burma was the first country to benefit from this innovated policy. The outstanding border differences were resolved, and a treaty of friendship and mutual non-aggression was signed in June 1960. It is significant to note that China practically accepted a delineation of the boundary as claimed by Burma... a delineation which constituted, with minor variation, the much-maligned McMahon line that Peking thereafter accepted as the "traditional customary line".[55]

With Indonesia, the Chinese quickly arrived at an arrangement for the implementation of the Dual Nationality Treaty. At the same time, they promptly acquiesced to the draconian measures against Chinese residents. With Nepal, the pattern of Burmese agreement was repeated—China accepting the traditional alignment of the border. To Cairo, Peking apologized and gave the remarkable explanation that the Syrian Communist, Khalid Bagdash, had spoken in China against Nasser at the invitation of the Chinese Communist Party and not the Government. Towards India too, an important initiative was taken at the beginning of 1960 to seek a compromise on the disputed border question. But the tension that had surged up in the country made it impossible for Nehru to strike a bargain with the Chinese.

The apparent interest in Asia was, however, not limited to only those countries who had opted for a policy of non-alignment. It was also directed towards the Asian nations who had hinged their fate on the West. In fact, in some ways, the aligned nations were more important objects of Chinese diplomacy than some of the non-aligned nations. With remarkable rapidity, attacks on Pakistan disappeared from the Chinese press ; even the U-2 incident was quietly passed over. Border differences were resolved, a trade agreement was concluded, and a general understanding was reached on diverse international issues. With Tokyo, China moved away from its previous line of not seeking any economic relations as long as political relations had not been normalized. In a statement made on 27 August 1960 to the head of the Japan-China Trade Promotion Association, Chou En-lai, though still insisting on establishing

55.   See Ambekar and Divekar, *op. cit.*, pp. 188-191.

trade relations on a government level, held out some hope of resuming economic relations on a private level.[56] By 1962, it became more than apparent that China was eager to develop economic relations even if it involved the total abandonment of her previous line that political and economic relations were inseparable, and even if it meant a retraction from the preceding position that Japan must break off diplomatic relations with Taiwan.[57]

Africa

Within the framework of rising Chinese interest in the third world, the African continent too became an important target of revolutionary and diplomatic manoeuvres. The process of decolonization had become too widespread, and the revolutionary resurgence had become too intense in the area to be ignored by China, who in the aftermath of the Sino-Soviet dispute was seeking friends in the third world.

The first significant sign of this rising interest was the wide coverage that was given to African developments, and the appearance of myriad articles underlining revolutionary potentialities of Africa. Perhaps the most conspicuous sign, however, was the view expressed to this effect in the secret bulletin of the Chinese Army. The Political Department of the Army wrote :

Africa is now both the centre of the anti-colonialist struggle, and the centre for the East and the West to fight for the control of the intermediary zone, so that it has become the key point of world interest. The general situation is the forced withdrawal of old colonialism from Asia, or at least a large part of Asia and the changing of the last battlefield to Africa.[58]

It is interesting to note, however, that the Chinese interest was not cluttered by ideological considerations. Most of the principal writings relating to the African scene were neither concerned with the role of the Communist parties, nor were

56. *Ibid.*

57. In 1963, Chen yi stated "China knows full well that at present Japan cannot break off diplomatic relations with Taiwan" ; cited by D. Petrov, "Japan and Mao's group's foreign policy", *International Affairs* (Moscow : No. 12, 1965), p. 30.

58. J. Chester Cheng *et al.* (ed.), *The Politics of the Chinese Red Army. A Translation of the Bulletin of Activities of the People's Liberation Army* (Stanford : 1966), p. 484.

they making any searching analysis of class struggle.   As late as July 1960, when Soviet analysts were already busy stressing the unreliability of the African national bourgeoisie and the need for independent working class action, the Chinese treatment of African resurgence stressed the prime importance of armed national struggle of which the bourgeoisie were considered an integral part.[59] In fact, the developments in Africa were compared to such resurgences as the Boxer rebellion, the Chinese revolution of 1911 and the movement of May 1919.[60]

If China laid principal stress on the national liberation movements, she did not ignore the eventual possibility of socialist revolutions in Africa. For she appeared to be convinced that in due course the "embryo of national people's revolution in these countries will become a genuine people's revolution, give rise to Marxists, form political parties of proletariat, and go towards socialist revolution".[61]

Guided by their own experience, the Chinese leaders were, first of all, attracted by countries where armed struggle was raging. For it was, in their view, the only effective method by means of which a clean break could be made with the imperialists. It is, therefore, not surprising that the Algerian armed struggle against the French took pride of place in Chinese revolutionary thinking. On numerous occasions, it was repeatedly stressed that the Algerian struggle had set a brilliant example for the liberation of the African people. Therefore, when the Algerian Provisional Government was set up in the autumn of 1958, it was immediately recognized, and no hesitation was manifested when economic and military assistance was sought from Peking. In fact, during the visits of different delegations representing the Provisional Government, detailed arrangements were believed to have been made for the financing of arms purchase in the Middle East and Eastern Europe, and for the training of selected Algerian officers in China.[62]

Peking also extended support to the guerilla war that was being waged by the *Union des Populations du Cameroun* in

---

59. *Ibid.*
60. *Ibid.*
61. *Ibid.*
62. *Revue militaire d'information* (Paris : April 1960).

Cameroon, and the national liberation movements in Angola and Mozambique.[63] Assistance was also given to elements in the Congo (Zaire) who, in the aftermath of Lumumba's assassination, had raised the flag of revolt in many provinces.

Collaterally, Peking established diplomatic relations with countries which had gained political independence. It made no discrimination, and was careful to cultivate state relations with all those who were willing to reciprocate. However, close diplomatic, economic and cultural relations were established with those African states who had—at least in the early sixties —developed an international reputation of belonging to the radical spectrum of African politics with a strong bias against the West. The most important of these were Ghana, Guinea, Mali, the United Arab Republic, Algeria, Burundi and Congo (Brazzaville). With all of them cultural agreements were signed and trade developed. And towards all of them, Peking had shown considerable skill in the application of its essentially limited funds and technicians. For example, in Burundi it established an embassy quite disproportionate in size to any normal interest in such a state.[64] An important commercial agreement was signed, as a result of which Chinese goods flooded the market. The leading personalities of Burundi were constantly invited to the Chinese Embassy, and according to one report, money was lavishly distributed.[65] The small state also became an important centre from which the Chinese kept close contact with the Congolese rebels.

In Congo (Brazzaville) the Chinese Embassy became the dominant force. Less than 18 months after the overthrow of President Youlou, the national revolutionary movement openly reflected China's foreign policy. More than 50 technical officials attached to the embassy were assigned, according to some reports, to work closely with a specific ministry or organization ranging from agriculture to children's groups.[66] In 1964, Peking gave a 5 million dollar loan to Brazzaville to help the

63. *New York Times* (Paris : 4 and 7 January 1964).
64. *Ibid.* (5 February 1965).
65. *La Tribune de Geneve* (Geneva : 29 June 1965).
66. *New York Times* (6-7 March 1965).

regime balance its budget ; and a year later, the latter accepted a 20 million dollar loan for setting up Chinese-run small industries. Each loan was interest-free and was for a period of 10 years.[67]

There were other areas too where Chinese influence became important. The island of Zanzibar, for example, to whom the Chinese gave important military and technical aid, and Somalia which came to depend heavily on Peking for economic and military assistance.[68]

Latin America

Chinese sights were also turned on Latin America. The flow of printed material was sharply increased, correspondents were despatched to a few countries to cover developments, and a Chinese-Latin American Friendship Association was created in Peking (1960) to promote Latin American travel to China.[69]

An important effort was made to establish diplomatic and trade relations with many Latin American states. But, apart from the establishment of diplomatic relations with Cuba and some trade relations with a few other countries, Peking's efforts in this domain were not successful. Most of the governments in the area were too conservative and too dependent on their big neighbour to cultivate relations with China. And some of those who were eager to achieve some disengagement from the United States did not see any political or economic advantage in cultivating with China. Peking thus did not have any great options in the field of inter-state relations, and was reduced to concentrating on Cuba. But in regard to this country too, Peking was unable to forge real and meaningful relations, in view of the fact that she had neither the military strength nor the economic power to meet the needs of that country.

Chinese activities in Latin America were thus principally devoted to the task of asserting influence on revolutionary

---

67. *Ibid.*
68. For details see John K. Cooley, *East Wind over Africa. Red China's African Offensive* (New York : 1968), pp. 23-46.
69. For details see E. Poppino, *International Communism in Latin America. A History of the Movement, 1917-1963* (London : 1964), pp. 173-189.

movements in the area. Undoubtedly, China had a distinct advantage over the Soviet Union on the question. In the first place, she was not inhibited in her revolutionary task. Not having any diplomatic relations with the Latin American states, she could openly side with revolutionary uprisings, whereas the Soviet Union, cluttered by economic and political factors, was inhibited in openly siding with the revolutionary movements. Secondly, the Chinese revolutionary strategy, centred around the peasants, appeared to be more appropriate to the Latin American conditions than the classical Soviet strategy centring around the working class.

From all this, it is apparent that Communist China had been able to establish meaningful political (diplomatic and revolutionary) and to some extent commercial relations with the third world. Practically everywhere she had been able to generate interest which no other Asian, African or Latin American country had been able to do. And, in almost all the developing countries, she had left a vital impact—a no mean achievement for a nation which only two decades earlier was struggling for her stability and survival.

Set-back in the third world

But all this did not last long ; for by the middle sixties, Peking's relations with the third world began to spiral downwards, leaving the middle kingdom once again in a state of complete isolation.

In Africa, the diminution of China's influence was perhaps most striking. The most advanced centre of Chinese activity expelled the Chinese diplomats because of the alleged involvement in the assassination of Burundi's Premier Pierre Ngendendume.[70] In West Africa, the governments of Niger, the Ivory Coast and Upper Volta formally issued joint (February 1965) warnings about the dangers of Chinese penetration in areas south of the Sahara.[71] The Presidents of Madagascar and Malawi also issued statements to this effect.[72] In Kenya, the

---

70. *New York Times* (5 February 1965).
71. Pierre Martens and Paul F. Smets, *Afrique de Pekin* (Brussels : 1966).
72. For details see E. Mendiaux, *L'Afrique sera Chinoise* (Brussels : 1965), *passim*.

National African Union—the only party authorized ʾto function
—decided (July 1965) in favour of breaking diplomatic relations
with China on the grounds that her embassy in Nairobi had
become a centre of subversive activity.[73] Even in the small state
of Congo (Brazzaville), where Chinese influence was fairly
strong, Peking received a serious set-back in 1965. The pro-
Chinese Prime Minister, Lissouba, was replaced by Nazazouloy
who represented the pro-Soviet tendency in the party. Other
leaders—including the President of the National Assembly, and
the Secretary of the trade unions—who were known for their
pro-Chinese views were also excluded.[74] The new Government
declined to take sides in the Sino-Soviet dispute, and refused to
modify her traditional relations with France.[75]

Perhaps the most important development was the series of
successful *coups d'etat* in West Africa. The *coups d'etat* in
Dahomey and the Central African Republic culminated in
the breaking of diplomatic relations with Peking.[76] The
one in Ghana—while Nkrumah was travelling in Peking—led to
the considerable decline of Chinese influence in the country,
including the closing down of some guerilla training camps.[77]

In Latin America too, China suffered some set-backs.
Cuba—the only Latin American state with whom China had
diplomatic relations—had abandoned her neutral posture in
the Sino-Soviet dispute, and had come out openly in favour
of the Soviet line. In March 1965, Cuba attended the Moscow
consultative meeting of the Communist parties. In September
of that year, China was attacked for distributing Chinese
propaganda material to Cuban army officers and government
officials..[78] Perhaps the most serious sign of deterioration in
Sino-Cuban relations was the Chinese decision to cut their
purchase of Cuban sugar, and the Cuban attack accusing the
Chinese of "brutal reprisals" of an economic nature for

73. *Le Monde* (30 July 1965).
74. *The Times* (London : 4 January 1966).
75. *Le Monde Diplomatique* (Paris : June 1966).
76. Pierre Martens and Paul F. Smets, *op. cit.*, pp. 77-81.
77. *Ibid.*
78. Ernst Halperin, "Peking and the Latin American Communists",
     The China Quarterly (January-March 1967), p. 148.

purely political reasons. In one of the bitterest exchanges among socialist states, Castro said that the Chinese were guilty of "hypocrisy, insolence, absolute contempt, betrayal of confidence, friendship and brotherhood".[79]

Among the Latin American Communist parties, Chinese influence had become minimal, and at the tricontinental conference held in Havana in January 1966, the Chinese were really isolated and were prevented by Cuban and Soviet skilful manoeuvres from making the conference a platform for their customary denunciation of revisionism.[80]

Even in Asia, where China, because of her geographical location, had exercised effective influence, her authority began to decline. With Indonesia, the relations atrophied after the abortive *coup d'etat* of the Communist Party of September 1965, leading to the mutual withdrawal of diplomats.[81] With Burma, they seriously deteriorated after the defiance by the young overseas Chinese of the rules and regulations of the Rangoon authorities.[82] With Cambodia, they took a turn for the worse after it became increasingly evident that the Chinese technical experts, intoxicated by the cultural revolution, were openly interfering in the internal affairs of the country.[83] And the Nepalese Government began to show signs of disengagement from Peking in the aftermath of pro-Maoist propaganda unleashed by Chinese technicians working on different projects.[84]

Even in the neighbouring Communist countries, Peking's influence significantly declined. By the beginning of 1965, the rapprochement between the Soviet Union and North Korea again began to develop, leading to the signature of the Defence Treaty of 1965. In Vietnam too, it became increasingly evident that the Chinese influence, in comparison to the

79. Quoted from the English translation of the Castro statement in *Peking Review* (25 February 1966).
80. For details see Albert-Paul Lentin, *La lutte tricontinentale. Imperialisme et revolution apres la conference de la Havane* (Paris : 1966), pp. 57-59.
81. For details see *Current Scene* (Hongkong : 4 November 1968).
82. *Le Monde* (28 June 1967).
83. *Ibid.* (16 September 1967).
84. *The Statesman's Weekly* (New Delhi : 26 August 1967).

Soviet influence, was on the decline.

What were the reasons for this apparent diminution of Chinese influence among the third world countries ? How is it that, notwithstanding the rapid acquisition of considerable economic power and military strength, China was unable to maintain her influence in the area ?

In the first place, the rapid deterioration of the internal situation, following the cultural revolution, was by no means conducive to the projection of a favourable image in the world. The indiscriminate attacks launched against foreign embassies, and the determination with which the Chinese technical advisers in foreign countries openly propagated "the thought of Mao Tse-tung" undoubtedly contributed to the decline of the Chinese image. But perhaps the most disquieting effect on the world was the myriad declarations, emanating from Peking. If Lin Piao was optimistically predicting the success of revolutionary upheavals—obviously of Chinese model—the communique of the 11th plenary session of the Eighth Central Committee of the Communist Party was calling upon people to struggle against the "imperialists" and the "reactionaries".[85]

Secondly, China, at the moment, is not a major power but only a regional one. She does not possess the military power or the economic strength to make effective moves in areas which happen to be remotely situated from the Chinese mainland. Africa and Latin America are the far away areas. Even parts of Asia, though geographically near, are none the less far enough to make it impossible for the middle kingdom to exercise any effective influence. Therefore, any political or military support that she might extend to her friends cannot have the same effectiveness as the assistance emanating from the Soviet Union or the United States. It can only be marginal.

Thirdly, Peking does not possess the economic power to give large-scale assistance, or develop important trade relations with the third world. The Chinese slogan of "self-reliance",

85. Foreign Languages Press, *The Decision of the Central Committee of the Chinese Communist Party concerning the Great Proletarian Revolution* (Peking : 1966).

though appealing, could not be pursued by the third world countries, in view of their rising economic needs which, for the time being, can be more easily met by the western countries and the Soviet Union. Even militantly leftist countries realized the need for developing or maintaining ties with the western world. Ghana, despite her allegiance to socialism under Nkrumah, sought foreign capital to accelerate her economic development. Algeria, notwithstanding her close political ties with Moscow and Peking, eagerly sought economic relations with France. And Guinea, in addition to her economic relations with the socialist countries, urgently felt the need to turn to Paris for aid and trade which France had suddenly stopped in 1958.

Fourthly, the Sino-Soviet dispute has made the task of Chinese diplomacy far more difficult than was the case before. For now she has to dissipate her limited power to contain not only United States influence, but also that of the Soviet Union. She now has to struggle to diminish not only the power of the "imperialists", but also that of the Soviet Union, whose image of progressiveness is still deeply ingrained in many countries. In fact, the myriad activities in the third world seem to suggest that she is at present more concerned with limiting Soviet influence than that of the United States. The declarations that have been made, the visits undertaken, and the numerous front organizations that have been created since 1964 have been primarily directed against the Soviet Union. For any nation, such an uphill and quixotic task would have resulted in dire consequences as in fact it did in the case of Germany during World War II. For a developing and deeply riven nation like China, it was simply disastrous. The ambitions apparently were totally unrelated to her ability.

Fifthly, in their zest to undermine Soviet influence, the Chinese Communists have introduced the Sino-Soviet dispute into all Afro-Asian solidarity conferences. Such tactics have ineluctably caused these conferences to degenerate into a Sino-Soviet wrangle in which important problems have been sidetracked. Naturally, this has not been to the liking of leaders from developing countries. For example, at the Afro-

Asian solidarity conference at Moshi (4-11 February) in 1963, despite all the appeals of the Soviet delegate to avoid public debate of divisive issues, the Chinese carried on a ruthless struggle against the "white" Soviet delegation. All this was received with great misgivings by many in Africa.[86] Again, at the tricontinental conference held in Cuba in January 1966, the Chinese attack against the Soviet Union was coldly received by most of the delegations.[87]

Lastly, the rapid nuclear development of China has probably generated a feeling of uneasiness among many developing nations—not because she has become nuclear but because she continues, unlike other nuclear nations, to belittle the dangerous consequences of a nuclear holocaust.

Post-Cultural Revolution phase

Thus by the middle and late sixties, China was left in a state of unparalleled isolation. Her influence—political and ideological—suffered such a serious retrogression that it seemed as if it might take years before she would be in a position to reassert herself in the Third World. But this, however, was not the case ; for by 1969—after the domestic convulsions had been brought under control—Peking returned to international diplomatic and trading arenas with vigour and imagination. Ambassadors, who had been withdrawn during the Cultural Revolution, have returned to their posts. China's trade has resumed its upward growth, and she has embarked upon her largest aid programme to date—the construction of the railroad from Tanzania to the Zambian copper fields.

Following the armed clashes in April 1969 over the disputed islands in the Ussuri River in Manchuria, Sino-Soviet relations have improved somewhat, and there are some indications that the two Communist giants plan an increase in their trade and are engaging in border talks. However, the most striking development has been the surge of international recognition that it is People's Republic of China and not the rival Republic of China in Taiwan which is the legitimate government of

---

86. Zbigniew Brezizinski (ed.), *Africa and the Communist World* (Stanford : 1963), p. 136.
87. Albert-Paul Lentin, *op. cit.*, p. 58.

China. The People's Republic has been admitted to the United Nations, a variegated group of nations have established diplomatic relations, including Canada, Italy, Ethiopia, Chile and Nigeria ; and a dialogue between Washington and Peking has been formally inaugurated with Nixon's visit to China.

What possible effect can all these developments have on China's relations with the Third World ? Would her tasks in the developing areas become easier now that she has gained significant recognition ? Or, on the other hand, would her objectives and effectiveness in the Third World be jeopardized now that she has to make global moves on the chessboard of world politics ? It is of course difficult to answer these basic issues with any exactitude, for the current international situation is too transitory and too complex to permit any sober assessment. None the less, if one were to compound some of the inherent difficulties mentioned in the preceding pages with the new fact that China, recently recognised as a major power, would have to further circumfuse her limited energies, one could venture to suggest that her task in the Third World would become more difficult than before.

Conclusions

Since her inception, Communist China has been firmly and irrevocably committed to the policy of bringing about a complete erosion of western influence in the Third World. Although she has been steadfast in the pursuit of this objective, the tactics she has employed to attain it have varied from time to time.

During the first three years after the revolution, the Chinese Communists relied on revolutionary tactics rather than on classical instruments of diplomacy. They openly encouraged the Communist parties of the newly independent countries to revolt against their own governments. When it became apparent that China was making no headway with such tactics, and that western influence continued to maintain its position, a new policy was adopted. This policy was two-pronged. One was a moderate and friendly diplomatic policy directed towards the expanding non-aligned world, with the specific purpose of slowly disengaging it from the West. The other was a revolutionary policy, seeking to create anti-Western sentiments among the Asian, African and Latin American people through front organizations.

This two-pronged policy against the West was continued with remarkable success until 1959. From that year onwards, however, China's policy was rendered less effective, for she then began to devote her limited power to the enormous task of containing not only United States influence, but also that of the Soviet Union—a task, as we have seen, infinitely more difficult. In fact, it is apparent today that with the escalation of the Sino-Soviet dispute, China has primarily turned her sights on the task of undermining Soviet influence in the third world.

The task was rendered even more difficult by the unleashing of the cultural revolution. Although it was a phenomenon that was principally concerned with the internal situation, it did not fail to erode further China's influence in the third world, leaving her in a state of unparalleled isolation in international affairs.

But this does not mean that in the not too distant future, China may not be able to extricate herself from the difficult situation, and reassert her influence in the third world. In fact some signs are already discernible.

In the first place, she has a great potential for becoming a great power. Notwithstanding the difficulties following the cultural revolution, she still possesses all the features that make a nation great and strong—a vast territory, immense population, an accelerated rate of economic growth, a growing military strength and an obsession to attain a great power status. No other nation among the developing countries has all these features, and no other nation of the third world is expected to acquire them in the foreseeable future. In fact, one could venture to suggest that China has already established the image of a great power among many nations of the third world.

Secondly, the manner in which the international economic situation is evolving is also favourable to China. One is witnessing the tragic spectacle of the world becoming sharply divided between the haves and the have-nots. The rich nations continue to become richer as the poor nations continue to become poorer. For the developing nations this great "alienation" of the 20th century is far more vicious and dehumanizing than is any gulf between the workers and the bourgeoisie in a capitalist society. If this trend continues—as appears likely—would this not give China an opportunity to seize the leadership of the third world? Furthermore, would this not encourage Africa, Asia and Latin America to turn to China, the strongest among them?

PART II

Chapter III

Soviet Union and India

WITHIN the general framework of rising Soviet interest in
Asia, there were obviously some countries which, by the very
nature of their size, population, strategic location and material
resources, were considered as principal targets of Soviet diplomacy. India naturally was one of them. However, the
generally negative Soviet view of the Asian process of decolonization in the middle forties made it hardly possible for them
to welcome the changes in India where political power was
transferred to the Indian National Congress in 1947.[1] What
is indeed remarkable is that, notwithstanding Nehru's first
declaration as Minister of External Affairs of the interim
government that the Soviet Union was India's neighbour with
whom "we shall have to undertake many common tasks and
have much to do with each other",[2] the Soviet reaction to
Indian independence was distinctly unfriendly.

The Mountbatten plan, under which independence was
given to India and Pakistan, was criticised, and the leadership
of the Congress Party was considered to have gone over to
reaction by agreeing to British terms for a political settlement.[3]
E. Zhukov, in an article on India, stated that the Indian
leadership had capitulated to imperialism because the big

1. For details about general Soviet policy towards Asia in the middle
   forties, see Chapter I.
2. *The Statesman* (30 September 1946).
3. *Izvestia* (Moscow : 5 July 1947).

bourgeoisie feared the masses more than they feared the British. Nehru, who had been regarded as a progressive liberal, was now accused of having moved to the right with such reactionary leaders as Patel.[4] Even Gandhi was not spared. His entire thinking was considered to be "the basic ideological weapon of the bourgeoisie for the subjection of the masses to their influence, and a prime brake on the awakening of the class consciousness of the workers".[5] The Indian policy of non-alignment was also condemned and was considered "to justify a policy of collaboration with English capitalism, a policy of establishing closer contact between the Indian bourgeoisie and English capitalism".[6]

As loyal adherents of the world Communist movement, the Central Committee of the Indian Communist Party changed the party line to fit it into the new global "cold war" pattern. In December 1947, the Central Committee bitterly excoriated the Indian bourgeoisie and castigated the Congress, including Nehru personally. And at the Second Party Congress, held in Calcutta in February 1948, a new political line was instituted which gave a revolutionary call to the working class to initiate a programme of reckless violence and insurrection with the clear-cut aim of overthrowing the existing Indian Government.[7]

Under the circumstances, it was hardly possible for the Nehru Government effectively to implement its policy of non-alignment; for this in effect required the existence of an international atmosphere, permitting not only the establishment of friendly relations with the existing blocs, but also the recognition by them of the existence of such a policy. Therefore, while formally continuing to adhere to a policy of non-alignment, the Indian Government apparently had no other choice but to move closer to the West, which, though equally critical

---

4. E Zhukov, "K polozheniiu v Indii", *Mirovoe Khoziaistvo i Mirivaia* (Moscow : July 1947), pp. 3-4.
5. A. Dyakov, *Natsionalny vopros i Angliisky Imperializm v Indii* (Moscow : 1948), p 33.
6. E. Zhukov, *loc. cit*, p. 4.
7. For details, see M. R. Masani, *The Communist Party of India* (London : 1954), pp. 89-90.

of non-alignment, was none the less eager to develop close relations with India in the hope of convincing the latter to ally herself with the West.

India's initial orientation to the West was also partially influenced by her close identification with political ideas emanating from that region. Notwithstanding the firmly ingrained opposition to imperialism and emotional attraction to the Soviet experiment, many of the decision-makers were attracted, influenced and even shaped by the paradigm of political and social ideas rampant in the capitals of liberal Europe. Even the deep attraction to socialism noticeable among many of them was incrusted with political liberalism, making it possible to communicate with the West European nations within a generally acceptable framework.

It was thus not at all surprising to discern a pro-Western orientation in India's external relations during the first few years after independence. For instance, her attitude to Korean unification and the Greek civil war was closer to that of the West than that of the Soviet Union.[8] Indeed, according to K.M. Pannikar, Indian policy on the two issues led the Soviet and the Ukrainian delegations in the United Nations to adopt a less cordial attitude towards their Indian counterpart.[9]

At a meeting of the Commonwealth Prime Ministers in October 1948, India gave her unequivocal support to Great Britain's decision to adhere to the association of West European nations under the Brussels Treaty. India's decision to continue her membership in the Commonwealth, and her agreement to give joint Commonwealth military aid to Burma for the obvious purpose of strengthening the existing government against the Communist rebels, were also important indications of New Delhi's partiality for the West.

However, in order to obviate the inevitable impression that India was slowly sliding into the Western camp, Nehru, at the same time, made it a point openly to express his anti-imperialist views. On numerous occasions he proclaimed that the

8. Karunakaran, *India in World Affairs* (Calcutta : 1952), p. 280.
9. K. M. Pannikar, *In Two Chinas. Memoirs of a Diplomat* (London : 1955), pp. 10-11.

colonial world must become independent, and actually assured
the nationalists of many subjugated countries of India's moral
and material support. Although there is no doubt that by
adopting such a policy Nehru was giving expression to his
genuine convictions against imperialism, one should none the
less not ignore the important fact that such open statements
served the purpose of convincing the outside world of India's
independence from the West. For instance, the convening of
an Asian conference by Nehru in 1949 to take concerted action
against the Dutch, who were trying to reimpose their rule in
Indonesia, must have gone a long way towards the projecting
of an anti-colonial image of India.

Thus, during the first two years of her independence, India
found herself in the position, on the one hand, of an anti-
imperialist nation eager to assist the colonial world in the
attainment of independence and, on the other, of establishing
meaningful economic and political relations with the West to
the exclusion of the Soviet Union.

With the communization of China, the relations between
India and the Soviet Union became even more strained. For
the Soviet leaders, the Communist revolution in China was
only a confirmation of the long-held view regarding the potentialities of Communist revolutions in Asia.

But if Moscow was impressed by the unexpected success of
the Chinese revolution, it was also perhaps fearful of the
important influence Communist China could exercise on the
Asian Communist parties. Such a possibility could not be
excluded in view of the apparent similarities existing among
the Asian nations which made the Chinese experiment more
relevant to Asian conditions than the one that was taking place
in the Soviet Union. An extra effort was therefore made to
be even more belligerent, in their criticism of Nehru and his
government. The Indian Prime Minister, who was visiting
the United States during the month in which the Chinese
revolution had taken place, was vehemently criticised by the
Soviet press. Explaining the implications of Nehru's remarks
in New York that India would support the United States in
any "defensive war", Dyakov said that "India was prepared
to offer all her resources to the Anglo-American bloc of insti-

gators of a further cold war".[10]

Another Soviet observer went even further and stated that "the vacancy left by Chiang Kai-shek is being offered to Nehru".[11]

For India, the dramatic events of China were hardly a favourable sign, for they had not only skewed the Asian balance of power in favour of the apparently monolithic Communist world, but had, with the Chinese occupation of Tibet, brought a dynamic and an unfriendly Communist state to the very doors of India. For the first time, the Himalayan region, which had remained dead all through history, suddenly became a live frontier, generating new strategic problems that the country had never faced before.

But what could India do in the light of the new situation? A formal alliance with the West was excluded, in view of the forthright decision of the Nehru Government to make non-alignment its article of faith. An alliance with the Communist world was equally impossible in view of the profound ideological and political gap that separated those who were in power in India from those who were the decision-makers in Communist countries.

None the less, it was obvious that some new and concerted action had become necessary so far as Communist countries were concerned, for the monolithic unity of the bloc seemed threatening ; and it was in response to this need that there arose a broad consensus among the Indian decision-makers to deploy different efforts to face the new situation.

First of all the Indian Communist Party, which had raised the flag of revolt against the Nehru Government, was ruthlessly suppressed. Obviously such firm action was considered vital in order to forestall the political degeneration of India. But it did not, at the same time, fail to impress on Moscow and Peking that the Indian decision-makers were in firm control of the country. Secondly, a number of administrative, police and military measures were taken to bring about an improvement in India's defences.[12] A concerted diplomatic offensive

10. *Pravda* (Moscow : 25 November 1949).
11. *New Times* (Moscow : 12 October 1949), pp. 20-21.
12. For details, see Lorne J. Kavic, *India's Quest for Security : Defense Policies, 1947-1965* (Berkeley : 1967), pp. 46-61.

was launched in order to normalize relations with Peking.[13] It was argued that China, geographically and spiritually closer to India, if properly manipulated might give greater precedence to Asian solidarity than to Marxist dogma.[14]

The results of the concerted Indian action were remarkably successful, for, not too long afterwards, one began to discern a slow but perceptible change in China's attitude towards India.[15]

Change in Soviet attitude

Within a year after the shift in Chinese policy, the Soviet Union too began to show definite signs of change. Evidently, it was hardly expedient for the Moscow leaders to continue the old and rather unsuccessful line when China, the largest and most powerful Communist nation in Asia, had decided to blaze a new and benign path. For one thing, it would have only further aggravated Soviet isolation from Asia, leaving the diplomatic field wide open for China to increase her influence in the area. For another, it would have generated serious differences among the Asian Communists who were already showing some signs of bemusement at the subtle manifestation of differences on the revolutionary strategy to be pursued in Asia.

Perhaps the most decisive reason that led to an innovation in Soviet policy, however, was the disastrous consequences that had resulted from the pursuit of the militant line. Almost all the Communist parties in the area had been crushed and isolated from the mainstream of Asian politics. In India, for example, where the Communist Party, over the years, had established impressive footholds among workers, peasants and intellectuals, the feckless revolts under the leadership of B.T. Ranadive and Rajeswar Rao—the one centring around the workers and the other around the peasants—plummeted their prestige to an all-time low, sharply declining the party's membership from an estimated 89,263 to 20,000.[16]

Such a serious set-back, both on the political as well as the

---

13. *Ibid.*, p. 46.
14. K. M. Pannikar, *op. cit.*, p. 123.
15. For details see Chapter IV.
16. Overstreet and Windmiller, *Communism in India* (Berkeley : 1959), p. 357.

diplomatic front, made it imperative for the Soviet leaders to re-examine their policy ; and it must have become evident to them that their assessment of the Asian political scene was largely influenced by the dichotomic situation in Europe, rather than the veritable political reality existing in the area. In the first place, many nationalist leaders and their political parties were too strong and too deeply rooted among the people of their countries to be overthrown by the artificially created revolutionary upheavals. And the Communist parties, though powerful enough to create confusion, were not effective enough actually to take over the reins of power. Secondly, many of the Asian leaders, having been impressed at some stage of their lives by the Soviet revolution, had often proclaimed their firm intention of introducing a much more far-reaching socialistic pattern of society in their countries than had ever been intended by the non-Communist leaders of the West Obviously this was in many ways a unique situation ; and a contemptuous identification of it with world capitalism had not only shown the magnitude of Soviet dogmatism, but had also exposed the lack of intellectual sophistication needed to understand new trends, new thoughts and new movements.

A rapid change was therefore instituted in Soviet ideological thinking and policy. Instead of striving for immediate control over these areas, Soviet diplomacy now limited its objective to the task of detaching them from the "imperialist bloc", and then slowly attaching them to the "camp of peace and socialism". The new trend in Soviet policy was therefore identified as "working with the national bourgeoisie" and it was more concerned with influencing the orientation of nationalist leaders in world affairs than encouraging their overthrow by the local Communist parties.

So far as India was concerned, the new line initially manifested itself in relatively minor matters. For instance, the Soviet Government, which had so far kept itself aloof, suddenly agreed in the beginning of 1952 to build a Russian pavilion at the International Industries Fair at Bombay, and expressed willingness to make capital goods available to India.[17] Indian business-

17. *India Record* (London : 28 February 1953).

men were unexpectedly invited to attend the International Economic Conference held in April 1952 in Moscow.[18] Stalin, who had not met any foreign diplomat for almost two years, granted a parting interview to the Indian Ambassador, Dr. Radhakrishnan, on 5 April of the same year.[19] And the Soviet Government promptly agreed to the appointment of K.P.S. Menon as the new Indian Ambassador to Moscow.[20]

The occurrence of such minor events in a non-Communist country may not be considered of any particular importance, but they are of significance in the case of the Soviet Union, where an important change is often preceded by a series of minor innovations. It was, however, the death of Stalin which heralded striking innovations in Soviet policy. More and more flexibility, imagination and vigour became apparent. Internally, the oppressive and harsh aspects of Stalinist legacy were quickly set aside, and externally a series of concrete diplomatic steps were taken to relax the suffocating tension that dominated the area.

So far as India was concerned, the first important and formal sign of Soviet change was manifested in August 1954, when Malenkov, in his speech to the Supreme Soviet, praised India's role in the Korean armistice.

The contrast in this speech between a severe criticism of the United States, and his friendly reference to the new states of Asia, gave a hint that the new Soviet leaders recognized the potential value of a friendly approach to the national governments of Asia.

The new Soviet Government lost no time in giving a concrete shape to its policy. In the summer of 1953, an Indian art exhibition was held in Moscow at the request of the Soviet Government.[21] In October 1953, the new Soviet Ambassador to New Delhi, M.A. Menshikov, handed a cheque of 296,560 rupees to Nehru for the national relief fund,[22] and placed a wreath on the tomb of Gandhi, an important gesture which his

18. *Ibid.*
19. *Ibid.*
20. K.P.S. Menon, *The Flying Troika* (London : 1963), p. 2.
21. *Ibid.*, pp. 17, 63.
22. *New Times* (Moscow : 31 October 1953), p. 32.

predecessor, Novikov, had carefully avoided. In the same month, he offered to supply India with industrial equipment, farm machinery and tools at prices more favourable than those prevailing in the West. In exchange for these commodities, Menshikov, on behalf of his government, agreed to buy jute and tea, for which there was at that time a great slack in demand in the West because of the Korean armistice. On 2nd December an important trade agreement was signed with India which bound the two governments to facilitate trade between the two countries over a wide range of goods.[23] Mutual visits were also encouraged between the two countries. By the end of 1954, as many as 14 Indian delegations, from a football team to industrialists, visited Moscow at the invitation of the Soviet Government.

India turns to Moscow

Undoubtedly, these events had created the necessary atmosphere for the growth of Indo-Soviet relations. All that was now needed was the development of some factors or circumstances which would push the relations between the two countries to a higher political plane. This was provided by the United States in 1954. During that year, Washington, in an effort to negate some of the inherent weaknesses apparent in Southeast Asia and the Middle East, devoted a considerable part of its efforts to the building up of military alliances. The Southeast Asia Collective Defence Treaty was signed on 8 September ; and under active encouragement from Washington, elements of the "Northern Tier" defence system, embracing Turkey, Pakistan, Iran and Iraq, also emerged in 1954. Furthermore, significant military assistance was furnished by Washington to Pakistan.

To New Delhi, the notion of a defence alliance to protect Southeast Asia and the Middle East against a possible Chinese or Soviet attack was abhorrent on many counts. First, such an alliance contradicted India's passionately held view that military blocs generally were steps towards war rather than peace. Secondly, the projected inclusion of Pakistan threatened to

---

23. For complete text, see *Foreign Affairs Reports* (New Delhi : December 1959).

introduce a system of military blocs into India's immediate neighbourhood, thus converting the Indian sub-continent into a theatre of cold war at the very time when New Delhi was making strenuous efforts to make it the centre of a "peace area". Thirdly, the prospect of United States military assistance to Pakistan threatened to strengthen that country not only in relation to the Soviet Union with whom she hardly had any quarrel, but also in relation to India with whom important issues were still outstanding. Therefore, despite all the assurances by the United States that military assistance to Pakistan was not and would not be directed against India, Nehru reaffirmed his wholehearted distaste for the whole project.

Inevitably, all these developments germinated important changes in India's policy towards the outside world. First, a wave of anti-American sentiment swept the country, alienating even an important element of Indian public opinion which was sympathetic to the United States. In fact, so intense was this feeling that even the relatively moderate Nehru government was affected by it—so much so that the United Nations was informally advised to remove its officers of American nationality stationed in Kashmir, since they were no longer considered neutral in the Kashmir dispute.[24]

Secondly, India began to devote a considerable part of her diplomatic efforts to bring together all like-minded Asian countries with the object of giving definite shape to non-alignment as an international force. There does not seem to be any doubt that the United States' activities in the area threw into relief, and each other's company, those nations which for one reason or another found it more convenient to occupy the no-man's land between the Western and the Communist blocs than to attach themselves to either.

Thirdly, India began to show definite signs of moving closer to Peking and Moscow, the most important indications of which were Nehru's visit to Peking in 1954 and his acceptance of the Soviet invitation to visit the Soviet Union.

24. *Ibid.* (20 March 1954).

Soviet offensive to cultivate with India

Moscow, equally opposed to American efforts to build anti-Communist alliances, naturally viewed Indian opposition as an excellent opportunity to cultivate with India and exploit the rising anti-American feeling that was manifesting itself in the country. Nehru' ssevere criticism of United States military aid to Pakistan did not go unnoticed. On the contrary, wide coverage was given to his views in the Soviet press. The Indian people, said a *Pravda* article, "cannot but be alarmed seeing the attempts to set up an aggressive bloc right on India's borders, which will invariably lead to the building of foreign bases and airfields on the territories of India's neighbours and to the militarization of those countries with which it is attempting to maintain closer relations".[25]

A massive offensive of friendship was thus launched; and Soviet writers, who only a few years earlier had made it a point to stress the unfortunate aspects of Indian life, now began to project a favourable image of the country. Suddenly they found that "everything in India attracts the artist's eye".[26] Those who in the past had written about India's slums and filthy streets now mentioned "the fine buildings which to this day are like a hymn of man's genius".[27] In an effort to create a proper atmosphere between the two countries, Soviet historians began to underline the great importance that was attached by Lenin to the revolutionary movement in India.[28] They also discovered that Afanasi Nikitin, a subject of the Tsar, had visited India in 1469-72. Since it was appropriate and timely to give him credit for this adventure, he was duly made a national hero. In the presence of the Indian Ambassador, a statue of Nikitin was unveiled in Kalinan in May 1955.[29] Mahatma Gandhi, who had so far been consistently condemned as reactionary in Soviet publications, was now praised for his progressive and important role in the national struggle.[30]

25. *Pravda* (27 September 1953).
26. *New Times* (7 August 1954), pp. 27-29.
27. *Ibid.*
28. *Pravda* (21 April 1954).
29. K.P.S. Menon, *op. cit.*, pp. 17, 115.
30. N.A. Bulganin and N.S. Khruschev, *Speeches during Sojourn in India, Burma and Afghanistan* (New Delhi : 1956).

It was perhaps in the diplomatic field that the change in Soviet policy was most striking. No longer was India's foreign policy considered to be tied to the apron strings of the West, and no longer was Nehru considered a reactionary serving the interests of the imperialists. On the contrary, Soviet official declarations and articles in the press were now full of praise for India and her approach to world problems. Hardly an occasion was missed to underline her important role in international affairs. During Nehru's visit to the Soviet Union in June 1955, the Soviet public was mobilized to give him a reception "for which there has been no parallel in Moscow before or since".[31] As a part of this diplomatic offensive, the Soviet Government extended complete support to India on the two foreign policy issues—Kashmir and Goa—that faced her in the middle fifties. Unlike the West, whose attitude on these issues was, to say the least, ambivalent, the Soviet Government came out openly and categorically on the side of India. This became evident during Khruschev and Bulganin's visit to India in 1955. For Khruschev, the Kashmir problem had already been resolved by the people of the area, and it was only a question of time before "Goa will free itself from foreign rule and will become an integral part of the republic of India".[32]

But such diplomatic action, though undoubtedly effective for generating a favourable Soviet image, was apparently not sufficient to encourage Indian orientation in the direction of Moscow. For India was inhibited in her goal of attaining real and effective disengagement from the West due to her excessive dependence on that area. Practically all her aid came from the West, and almost all her trade was geared to western markets. The Indian leaders were aware of the difficulties that such a situation created in the formulation of an independent foreign policy, but they could hardly remedy this state of affairs in view of Soviet aversion to non-aligned India. Thus, notwithstanding the Indian determination to pursue an independent policy, her options in real terms were severely circumscribed. She could hardly disengage herself from the West.

However, after the death of Stalin, and with the inauguration

31. For some details, see K.P.S. Menon, *op. cit.*, p.106.
32. N.A. Bulganin and N.S. Khruschev, *op. cit.*, p. 73.

of a moderate policy, the forging of economic links with India and other non-aligned countries became the key lever of Soviet foreign policy.

An unprecedented Soviet offensive was launched to make India less dependent on the West. It was argued that as long as she was economically tied to the West, it was not possible for her to pursue an independent line on foreign affairs.

The net result of this offensive was the considerable rise in trade turnover between the two countries, From a negligible figure of 8.1 million rupees, it increased to 719.7 million rupees in 1961, to 1753.6 million in 1965,[33] to 2269.5 million in 1966-67,[34] and to 4970 million rupees at the end of 1968.[35] According to the commercial agreement for 1966-67, signed on 7 January 1966, the trade between the two countries was expected to double by 1970 as compared to 1964.[36] In fact, it has been suggested by some specialists that India could "hopefully increase her turnover of trade to more than double", as compared to 1964, "if she can harness and develop capacity to produce various items needed in the Soviet Union".[37]

It is evident that there was a favourable constellation of factors that contributed to this rapid rise : there was the Soviet determination to develop relations, and there was also the fact that the rapid rate of growth was accounted for by the low level from which it had started fifteen years earlier. None the less the rate of growth is too significant to be attributable only to the absence of any relations in 1953 or to such elements as political determination.[38]

In the case of aid too, the Soviet contribution to Indian economic development is undoubtedly significant. By 1967, Soviet

33. For details, see Yearbook of International Trade Statistics 1965 (New York : 1967), p. 361.
34. The Statesman's Yearbook 1968-1969 (New York : 1968), p. 381.
35. B.R. Bhagat, "Indo-Soviet Trade. Promising Prospects Ahead", Commerce (11 April 1970).
36. Soviet News (London : 11 January 1966), p. 23.
37. Government of India, India's Trade with East Europe (New Delhi : 1966), p. 45.
38. For details, see V. Rymalov, La collaboration economique de l'URSS avec les pays sous-developpes (Moscow ; not dated).

credits totalled well over 10 billion rupees and made India the recipient of by far the largest amount of Soviet foreign aid (exclusive of arms). Admittedly the total assistance emanating from Moscow is less than the aid given by Washington, but its impact on the Indian economy is undoubtedly greater. By and large, most Indians tend to agree with the view that the aid coming from Moscow is more favourable and more approximate to Indian economic thinking.

Although such a widely prevalent view may be partly due to the remarkably well-organized publicity concerning Soviet economic assistance, it is, however, principally due to the considerable advantage that accrues from such aid.

In the first place, Soviet assistance is primarily concentrated on heavy industry in the public sector—an area to which the Indian decision-makers have given top priority. In fact, most of the expansion of Indian heavy industry has been due to the direct or indirect assistance emanating from Moscow. Even a cursory glance at the Indian economic plans would show that Soviet assistance is concentrated on the building up of steel plants, on the exploring and refining of oil and on the development of heavy engineering and electrical equipment plants.[39]

Secondly, most of the credits given to India are long-term credits, the repayment of which begins one year after the completion of deliveries of the equipment.[40] Such an arrangement made it possible for India to incorporate Soviet assistance in her planning and establish her plans for a number of years. Thirdly, all the Soviet credits do not exceed an interest of 2.5 per cent. Fourthly, the repayment of Soviet credits is either in rupees or in goods.

The Soviet contribution to long-term Indian economic development is indeed significant, and it has played a decisive role in the forging of close and meaningful ties between the two countries. This was naturally considered as an important development by most Indians, as it implied not only a general Communist approbation of India's policy of non-alignment, but it also permitted her to decrease her dependence on the West, and

39. Ibid.
40. Ibid.

thereby successfully attain a balance between the East and the West without being criticised by either of them that she had slidden into the other camp.

Moscow and the Sino-Indian dispute

The general Communist approbation of India's foreign policy, however, did not last long; for by 1959 it became increasingly evident that Communist China was veering away from a gradualist and moderate policy in internal as well as external affairs. Internally, the "hundred flowers" movement that was launched by the Chinese leadership to generate free discussion was abruptly ended in 1958, and externally more and more emphasis was laid on the decisive shift of the international balance of power in favour of the Communist countries, on the unchanging character of United States policy to dominate the world, and on the relevance of "uninterrupted revolutions" in the developing countries.

As an integral part of this belligerent line, India was made an important target of Chinese hostility. A number of Indian political parties were accused of fomenting the Tibetan revolt of March 1959, and the Indian Parliament was denounced for interfering in the internal affairs of China.[41] An unusually long editorial appeared in the *People's Daily* on 6 May in which, alternating between condescending friendliness and outspoken intransigence, Nehru was criticised for his views on Tibet.[42] For the first time (January 1959) the entire border alignment between India and China was questioned, and in September of the same year, after some frontier incidents, a claim was laid to about 50,000 square miles of what the Indians considered to be a part of their territory.[43] Within a year after these developments, the relations between Peking and New Delhi had become so strained that they had begun openly to accuse each other of imperialistic designs. A new situation had thus developed.

41. *Peking Review* (31 March 1959).
42. The editorial was entitled "The Revolution in Tibet and Nehru Philosophy" ; for complete text, see *Tibet Documents* (New Delhi : 1959).
43. Indian Ministry of External Affairs, *White Paper* No. 11 (New Delhi : 1959), p. 53.

A general feeling of apprehension soon arose in India about the possible Soviet reaction to the dispute. For how could she, many argued, remain neutral in a conflict between a Communist and a non-Communist country? Therefore, when the Sino-Indian relations had become particularly tense as a result of the Longju incident in August 1959, it was widely assumed that Moscow would support Peking, thus recreating a common hostile front against India on the same lines as had existed during the first five years of Indian independence. However, to the surprise of many observers, the Soviet leaders adopted a line of neutrality. Through a *Tass* statement of 9 September 1959, the Soviet Government deplored the Sino-Indian dispute, and expressed the hope that it would be settled through peaceful negotiations between the two states.

Such a view was reiterated by Khruschev personally. Speaking at a meeting of the Supreme Soviet on 31 October 1959, he regretted the incidents between states "friendly to us" and stated that "we would be very happy if there were no more incidents, if the existing frontier disputes were settled through friendly negotiations to the satisfaction of both parties".[44]

Such an attitude on the part of the Soviet Government was indeed unprecedented; for never since the formation of Communist states in Eastern Europe and the Far East had Moscow adopted a posture of neutrality between a Communist and a non-Communist state.

What was it that led the Soviet leaders to adopt such an unusual attitude? Why did they decide upon such a non-committal posture, when it was unobtrusively evident that any public expression of neutrality would only introduce another element of strain in the already aggravated relations with Peking?

It would appear that there were two important considerations that may have led the Soviet Government to adopt such an unusual attitude. First, by 1959 Soviet policy towards the non-aligned world had become remarkably successful. It had by that year not only succeeded in establishing economic relations and forging useful political links, but it had success-

44. N. S. Khruschev, *World Without Arms, World Without Wars*, Book 2 (Moscow : 1959), p. 399.

fully disengaged many of them from the West—an important Soviet objective. Naturally the Soviet Government was reluctant to undo all these achievements—which might have been the case if they had criticised India on the Sino-Indian border dispute. Secondly, by 1959, Sino-Soviet differences had bubbled to the surface. On many important political and ideological issues a point of no return had already been reached, and there were definite indications that China and Soviet Russia had decided to go their different ways. Under the circumstances, Moscow was unlikely to risk losing its already enhanced prestige among the non-aligned countries in order to appease China who was, in any case, determined to go her own way irrespective of the stand Moscow might take on the Sino-Indian dispute. Therefore, despite the informal appeals from Peking that Moscow should refrain from any public declaration that might embarrass China, the *Tass* statement was made.[45]

None the less, it is evident that the conflict between New Delhi and Peking must have been a source of great concern and embarrassment to the Soviet leaders. Clearly any further escalation of the dispute was not in their interest, for it would have further narrowed their margin of manoeuvrability and would probably have contributed to the undermining of their policy of building bridges towards the West as well as the non-aligned countries. It is therefore not suprising that notwith-standing Sino-Soviet differences, Khruschev, during his un-expected and rather sudden visit to India on 11 February 1960, discussed the Sino-Indian border dispute extensively with the Indian leaders, and finally persuaded reluctant Nehru to extend an invitation to Chou En-lai to discuss Sino-Indian differences.[46] However, in the prevailing state of public opinion in India—including Nehru's own party—it was not possible for the Prime Minister to conduct negotiations with Chou En-lai on a give-and-take basis. The Chinese proposal of surrendering the Indian claim over Aksai Chin area in lieu of Chinese recognition of the McMahon line was rejected, leading to the further exacerbation of the Sino-Indian dispute.

45. *Peking Review* (8 November 1963).
46. *Hindu* (13 February 1960).

With the further deterioration of Sino-Indian relations, Moscow went even further and began to criticise Peking for its attitude towards India. In an interview with the Moscow correspondent of the Indian Communist Party weekly, *New Age*, Khruschev suggested, in his flamboyant manner, that China's policy was incorrect, and compared it with that of the Soviet Government which had given away some of its territory to Iran to settle the border dispute with her southern neighbour.[47] According to the Chinese sources, the Central Committee of the Soviet Communist Party had informed the Chinese party in a verbal notification that "one cannot possibly seriously think that a State such as India which is militarily and economically immeasurably weaker than China would really launch a military attack on China and commit aggression against it".[48]

However, when the Chinese Communists launched their massive attack on India on 20 October 1962, Moscow made a *volte face* and squarely sided with the Chinese. In an editorial on 25 October 1962, *Pravda* denounced the McMahon line as a line imposed by the imperialists, and approved the Chinese ceasefire proposals.[49]

What were the reasons for this sudden and unexpected change ? Was it because the pro-Peking elements had suddenly gained the upper hand, or was it because the Soviet leaders, seriously embroiled in the Cuban crisis, were eager to avoid a showdown with Peking at that time ? Whatever might have been the reasons for such a radical shift, one thing was certain : India was deeply disappointed. Many members of the Parliament criticised the Soviet reaction to the dispute. Even E. V. Baliga, President of the National Council of the Indo-Soviet Cultural Society, deplored the stand taken by the Soviet Government.[50]

The Indian Government, however, did not give up hope that Moscow might change its attitude once the Cuban crisis had subsided. Therefore, despite the existence of general

47. *Link* (15 August 1962), p. 73.
48. Editorial Department of *People's Daily*, "The truth about how the leaders of the CPSU have allied themselves with India against China", *People's Daily* (2 November 1963).
49. *Pravda* (25 October 1962).
50. *Background* (New Delhi : 10 December 1962), p. 2.

discontent in the country, Nehru avoided criticising Moscow, and actually went to the extent of stating that he understood the Soviet difficulties on the question.   He said :

> The Soviet Union has been, as the House knows, consistently friendly to us. It has been put in a very difficult position in this matter because they (the Soviets) have been and are allies of China, and hence the embarrassment to them as between a country with which they are friendly and a country which is their ally. We have realized that and we do not expect them to do anything which would definitely mean a breach over there. It is not for us to suggest to any country. But we have had their goodwill and good wishes all along, even very recently, and that is a consolation to us and we certainly hope to have that in the future.[51]

On 5 November, however, the Soviet Government reverted to its original neutralist line. In an editorial on the border question, *Pravda* now maintained a complete silence about the McMahon line and no longer extended complete support to the Chinese ceasefire proposal. A simple appeal was made to both sides instead, to agree to a ceasefire and to discuss the whole question without imposing any conditions.[52]

With the further aggravation of the Sino-Soviet dispute, Moscow even renounced its posture of neutrality, and began openly to criticise China for her attitude towards India. At the Italian Communist Party Congress, held in December 1962, F. Kozlov criticised the Chinese Party for what he called an "adventuristic position" on the Sino-Indian border conflict.[53] In a series of articles in August 1963, *Pravda* denounced Chinese aggression against India, and lashed out at Peking's failure to seek a peaceful settlement of the border dispute.[54] On 15 February 1964, Suslov in his report to the plenary session of the Central Committee of the Soviet Communist Party also criticised Chinese policy towards India and viewed it as having

51.   Ministry of External Affairs, *Prime Minister on Chinese Aggression* (New Delhi : 1962), p. 87.
52.   *Pravda* (5 November 1962).
53.   *New York Times* (4 December 1962).
54.   *Pravda* (10 and 13 August 1963).

"rendered a great service to imperialism and done great harm to the national liberation movement, the progressive forces of India and the entire front of the anti-imperialist struggle".[55]

At the same time, Soviet aid was stepped up and a number of agreements were signed covering specific projects. The most important agreement was the Soviet accord in January 1965 to construct the Bokaro Steel Plant which the United States Government had agreed to build, but was forced to renounce later due to internal political pressures.[56]

It was, however, in the military field that the tempo of Soviet aid was really accelerated. Following the Chinese invasion, the Soviet Union sent all types of armed equipment needed for mountain warfare, agreed to establish factories to manufacture MIG-21 jet fighters, and made available ground-to-air missiles, light tanks, mobile and fixed launching installations and radar equipment which could be used on any part of the Indian frontier. By May 1964, the total military aid that emanated from Moscow—130 million dollars—was greater than the aid that was given by the United States during the same period.[57] And in September 1964, India received a new pledge of 140 million dollars under which the Russians agreed to supply 44 MIG-21s, 50 ground-to-air missiles, about 70 light tanks, 6 submarines and an assortment of various infantry weapons.[58] To finance this, the Russians provided a ten-year loan at 2 per cent.

Moscow and the Indo-Pakistan dispute

It is thus evident that within the general framework of Soviet diplomacy in Asia, India gradually acquired a significant place. In fact, one could venture to suggest that she had by 1964 gained a position of centrality. The quantum of military and economic assistance emanating from Moscow had indeed become considerable ; and the political encouragement she had begun to receive to attain some of her foreign policy objectives was as striking

55.   *Pravda* (3 April 1964).
56.   O. P. Mehrotra. *From Bhilai to Bokaro* (New Delhi : 1968).
57.   *New York Times* (13 May 1964).
58.   *Ibid.* (4 August 1965) ; see also *Link* (20 and 27 September 1964).

as the absence of such assistance from the United States and Great Britain.

However, after the fall of Khruschev in 1964, who was the real architect of excessive Soviet involvement in India, the new Soviet leaders adopted a remarkably subtle policy of extricating themselves from a position of immoderate involvement in any one country which was not under their direct control, and strove to develop relations with all nations who had successfully manifested a measure of assertiveness in international affairs. There was of course Japan with her vital economic power with whom political and economic relations were developed. There was Indonesia with her vast population, strategic location and important natural resources with whom, despite the military take-over in September 1965, important relations were maintained. And there were Iran and Turkey and Malaya, allies of the western world, who had become important objects of Soviet moderate diplomacy.

Perhaps the most significant development in this direction, so far as India was concerned, was the remarkable and rather rapid improvement in Soviet-Pakistan relations. Although some contacts had already been established in the early sixties,[59] effective signs of a real normalization, however, became evident only in 1964 and 1965. In 1964, a cultural agreement was signed, visits were exchanged, economic relations were developed, a Soviet loan was given and favourable articles were published in the Soviet press underlining the positive nature of developments in Pakistan.[60] In 1965, Ayub Khan visited the Soviet Union. This was the first time that the head of the Pakistan state had visited Moscow. Naturally the occasion was fully used to have an extensive exchange of views which resulted in the partial removal of misunderstandings that plagued the relations between the two countries.[61] But the principal

59. An aid agreement was signed with Pakistan in March 1961 and a trade agreement was concluded in August 1963.
60. For details, see I. H. Qureshi (ed.), *Foreign Policy of Pakistan, An Analysis* (Karachi : 1964) ; see also Mohammed Ahsen Chaudhri, "Pakistan's Relations with the Soviet Union", *Asian Survey* (California : September 1966), pp. 492-500.
61. For details, see Mohammed Ayub Khan, *Friends not Masters : A Political Autobiography* (London : 1967), pp. 168-174.

development in Soviet-Pakistan relations was the Soviet decision
to adopt a position of neutrality on the issue that racked the
two countries.   This became apparent during the Indian President's visit in September 1964.[62]   On this occasion, the joint
statement produced no mention of Kashmir.   During Prime
Minister Shastri's visit in the spring of 1965, the Soviet leaders
avoided taking a pro-Indian stand on Kashmir and the Rann of
Kutch disputes, and expressed the view that "the Soviet people
would like them to settle their border disputes and other
disputes peacefully, and all prerequisites for this are there".[63]
Two days later Kosygin noted that only imperialists could benefit
when "liberated states quarrelled", while the joint communique
omitted specific references both to Kashmir and the Kutch
issues, and declared eliptically that disputes "must be resolved
by way of peaceful talks and the use of force to settle disputes
is impermissible".[64]

By adopting such a policy, the Soviet Union succeeded in
disengaging herself from the Indo-Pakistan dispute in which
she had overly embroiled herself in the mid-fifties.   But this
disengagement could not in any way be likened to the policy
she followed after the independence of the sub-continent ; for
at that time she did not appear to be interested in forging
meaningful relations with either of the two governments, whereas in the mid-sixties she was eager to develop relations with
both of them.

The skilful handling of a complicated and rather explosive
situation stood the Soviet Government in good stead ; for not
too long after the adoption of such a line, it was successful in
establishing friendly relations with Pakistan without generating
a serious crisis in Indo-Soviet relations, without arousing the
indignation of sensitive India.   Undoubtedly, this was a remarkable feat of Soviet diplomacy.

With the rising interest of the Soviet leaders in the whole of
the Indian sub-continent, it became increasingly evident that
they were not prepared to limit their diplomatic actions to the
simple task of forging meaningful links with the two rivals. For

62. *Soviet News* (21 September 1964).
63. *Ibid*. (17 May 1965).
64. *Ibid*., p. 90.

it became increasingly evident that the effective advancement
of Soviet interest on the sub-continent as well as in the rest of
Asia was closely linked with the amelioration of relations
between India and Pakistan. Soviet diplomacy, therefore,
moved forward and began to express concern over the manner
in which the relations between the two countries continued to
deteriorate. At first, however, the concern was limited to the
simple task of making general statements stressing the urgency
of finding "a way towards the ending of bloodshed and conflict".[65]   But when the dispute finally exploded in the actual
outbreak of hostilities in September 1965, Moscow initiated an
important offensive to limit the conflict. Pressure was put on
both sides to avoid taking any action that might escalate hostilities, and severe objections were raised to the Indian decision
to open a new front in the Punjab area in order to relieve
Pakistani pressure on the Kashmir front.[66]   At the same time,
the Soviet Union warned the Chinese, who had the clear
intention of keeping the pot boiling,[67] not to exacerbate the
situation "as many states might find themselves drawn into the
conflict one by one".[68]

The Soviet leaders, however, knew that the best guarantee
against any further escalation evidently was the rapid termination of the conflict. And it is on this difficult task that they
set their sights ; informal diplomatic contacts were established
with the leaders of the two countries in order to impress upon
them the vital importance of peace in the area. Appeals were
promptly despatched to the two countries urging them to
"display realism, restraint and understanding of the grave consequences of the development of the armed conflict" ;[69] and
specific proposals were formally made to both Shastri and
Ayub Khan to meet in the Soviet Union. Kosygin personally

65. *Pravda* (24 August 1965).
66. Hari Ram Gupta, *Indo-Pakistan War, 1965*, Vol. 2 (Delhi : 1968),
    p. 217.
67. The Chinese had sent an ultimatum to India on 16 December "to
    dismantle all its military works for aggression on the Chinese side";
    for details, see Ministry of External Affairs, *Documents on China's
    Ultimatum to India* (New Delhi : 1966), p. 12.
68. *Soviet News* (14 September 1965), p. 113.
69. *Ibid.* (8 September 1965), p. 101.

offered his good offices to bring a rapid end to the conflict.[70]

At first there was reluctance from both sides, but when it became increasingly evident that the conflict was beginning to take on dangerous proportions, the leaders of the two countries finally agreed to meet in Tashkent. And it was in that important city of Central Asia that an agreement was concluded on 10 January 1966.[71]   Both governments agreed to resume normal relations and undertook "not to have recourse to force and settle their disputes through peaceful means".[72]   It is no exaggeration to state that without the active participation of Kosygin in the discussions, the agreement would not have been concluded.   In fact, it is known that the talks would have broken down, but for the last-minute Soviet intervention.[73]

Moscow had thus succeeded where the other powers had failed ; and she became—because of this remarkable feat—an important factor in Indo-Pakistan relations, perhaps more than the other major powers. But if Tashkent was a major diplomatic achievement for the Soviet leaders, it was also an eye-opener for them. The problems that racked Indo-Pakistani relations were too intractable and too forlorn to be resolved by good offices or through the mediatory efforts of a foreign power. The rapidity with which the two nations had quickly set aside the Tashkent agreement, and had nullified "the Tashkent Spirit", was a clear proof of the despairing situation that prevailed in the area.

Under the circumstances, the Soviet leaders slowly disengaged themselves from the position of seeking a meaningful solution to the conflict, and appeared to move towards the limited task of forestalling the violent explosion of the dispute. Apparently, the risks in such a situation were too great, and Moscow did not wish to stake its prestige, power and influence to resolve what appeared to be a forlorn conflict.

70. *Ibid.* (20 September 1965), p. 125.
71. For details, see M. S. Rajan, "The Tashkent Declaration : Retrospect and Prospect", *International Studies* (July-October 1966), pp. 1-28.
72. *Ibid.*, p, 101.
73. Tang Tsou (ed.), *China's Policies in Asia and America's Alternatives* (Chicago : 1968), p. 416.

The adoption of such a policy was also full of many pitfalls, and contained within itself dangerous germs of negating the very objectives for which it had originally been adopted, namely the goal of continually increasing influence in the two countries. Having once decided to maintain and develop relations with the two contending nations, Moscow found itself increasingly obliged to adopt policies that vitiated the development of relations with both of them.

The Soviet decision to give military assistance to Pakistan is a case in point. Up to the middle sixties, all the efforts of the Pakistan Government to obtain military assistance from Moscow were firmly resisted by the Soviet leaders. But it soon became apparent that the continuous hedging on such an important issue was generating a difficult situation for the Soviet Government.

In the first place, it was leading to a continual manifestation of discontent in Pakistan, thereby creating a situation where the continuous growth of Soviet-Pakistan relations was being jeopardized. Obviously, the Soviet Government, after having successfully developed relations with Rawalpindi, did not wish to see them undermined.

Secondly, a continuous refusal to give arms to Pakistan permitted the leaders of that country to insist in their negotiations with the Russians that they must in this case cease to give military assistance to India. Obviously, the Soviet leaders did not wish to accept such a proposal as it would have seriously affected Indo-Soviet relations. It was therefore considered that the making of a symbolic arms deal with Pakistan would permit them to maintain their bridges with that country without seriously jolting their relations with India. A decision was thus taken in July 1968 to give military aid to Pakistan.[74]

What were the factors that brought about this change in the Soviet attitude towards the Indian sub-continent ? Why did the Soviet leaders decide to equate Pakistan with India on certain matters ?

In the first place, there appeared to have developed, since

74. For background information, see Mohammed Ayoob, "Soviet arms aid to Pakistan", *Economic and Political Weekly* (19 October 1968).

1964, a general trend in Soviet diplomacy to extricate itself
from an immoderate involvement in intractable problems which
are of no direct concern to Soviet interests. In the Pakistan-
Afghan dispute on the Pakhtoon question, the Soviet Union
ceased to side openly with Afghanistan. On the Cyprus issue,
the previous Soviet position of extending unconditional support
to the Cypriot Government against Turkey was slowly and
subtly abandoned ; and on the Indo-Pakistan dispute a position
of neutrality was adopted. The pursuit of such a political line
is not only a striking example of the growing sophistication in
Soviet diplomatic behaviour, but is perhaps an important sign
of a Soviet consensus that such a line, under the circumstances,
is the only effective way to safeguard Soviet national interests
and, at the same time, aggrandize Soviet influence.

Secondly, by the early sixties, India had ceased to carry any
great weight in international affairs. The humiliating Indian
defeat in the Sino-Indian war of 1962 was a brutal exposure of
her weaknesses and her inability to defend her interests and her
security. It became evident that she did not have the necessary
political and military strength to withstand an attack from the
outside. For the Soviet Union, which was obviously seeking
an effective counterbalance to the rising Chinese influence in
the area, the timid Indian performance must have been a source
of great disappointment, and was probably instrumental in
encouraging her to jettison her rather special relations with
India.

Thirdly, Pakistan, having partially disengaged from the
West, following a realization that none of her foreign policy
objectives had been achieved in co-operation with the West, had
begun to show increasing signs of seeking a rapprochement
with China. Border differences between the two countries had
been resolved by March 1963, important trade agreements had
been concluded in January 1963, and a general understanding
had been reached on diverse international issues including,
according to some reports, on some military matters.[75]

75. The Pakistan Foreign Minister, Bhutto, in fact implied that China
    would come to Pakistan's assistance in the event of an attack from
    India. For text of the speech, see K. Sarwar Hasan (ed.), *Docu-
    ments on the Foreign Relations of Pakistan : China, India, Pakistan*
    (Karachi : 1966), p. 377.

Apparently the drift of Pakistan in the direction of China must have been a source of great concern to the Soviet Union which was making all efforts to isolate the middle kingdom. And in order to forestall this development, Moscow must have felt the necessity of seeking a rapprochement with Pakistan

But this effort to develop friendly relations with Pakistan did not of course mean that India ceased to be an important objective of Soviet diplomacy. Far from it. Though having lost her position of centrality, India was still considered important. Economic and military assistance continued to flow. In fact, while appealing for peace during the Indo-Pakistan conflict of 1965, Moscow declined to impose an embargo and publicly stated in the Security Council that Kashmir was an integral part of India.

None the less, the changed Soviet attitude did not fail to create rumblings of discontent in India, generating for the first time a serious crisis in Indo-Soviet relations. The opposition in the Parliament—with the exception of the Communists—vigorously condemned the Soviet decision to give arms to Pakistan. Some of the leading members of the Congress Party were also critical. The Secretary of the Congress Parliamentary Party expressed the view that the "Soviet decision indicated that she (Soviet Union) attached more importance to friendship with Pakistan, for it was strategically placed".[76] The attitude of the Indian press was also critical, leading some to suggest that an effort ought to be made to defreeze relations with China in order to counter Soviet action.[77]

The attitude of the Indian Government was, however, cautious. After having made a number of discreet and vain efforts to dissuade Moscow from taking such a decision, some members of the Central Government, according to some reports, manifested their irritation by leaking the news to the Indian press. It was calculated that "a popular outburst" that would inevitably result from such a leakage would not be a bad idea and might actually persuade the Soviet leaders to renege from their

76. *National Herald* (New Delhi : 10 July 1968).
77. For details, see "Nireekshak", "What then must we do", *Economic and Political Weekly* (27 August 1968).

original decision.[78]   At about the same time, the Indian Prime Minister, Mrs. Gandhi, publicly reacted by stating that "we are not happy" about the Soviet decision, though she prudently made it clear that Indian foreign policy would not undergo any change.[79] The Defence Minister went a little further and expressed the view that the Soviet Union and the United States were making a "wrong assessment" of Pakistan by the supply of arms to her, thus leading her to adopt a "more intransigent attitude towards India".[80]

The Indian prudence was dictated by a number of very practical reasons to which sufficient importance has not been given. In the first place, it was simply not possible for the Indian Government to rock the boat of Indo-Soviet relations at a time when India was heavily dependent on the Soviet Union on a number of issues of foreign policy; for the dangerous consequences that would have resulted from such an action would have, in all probability, outweighed the advantages—if any—that India would have gained from such a policy. Secondly, the government of India had been repeatedly assured by Moscow that whatever arms the Soviet Union might supply to Pakistan would pose no danger to India.[81]   On the contrary, argued the Soviets, with arms supplies, the Soviet influence over Pakistan would increase and this would undoubtedly be used to discourage military adventures. Thirdly, most of the sophisticated military hardware that India received from the outside emanated from the Soviet Union ; and most of the financial and technical assistance also came from that country.

In view of all this, what could India do and from whom could she obtain military hardware, if she defied Moscow ? Military aid from the United States and Great Britain was no longer possible in view of their decision to stop all such assistance after the Indo-Pakistan war of 1965. Nor was it possible —at least at the moment—for her to normalize her relations

78.   From *Indian Express*, cited in *ibid.*
79.   *The Statesman's Weekly* (13 July 1968).
80.   *Ibid.* (23 November 1968).
81.   Kosygin made a statement to this effect in Calcutta on 10 September 1969. See *The Statesman's Weekly* (13 September 1969).

with Pakistan and China, for the conflicts with the two countries were too aggravated and too forlorn to be resolved easily.

India was thus left with no options, and had apparently no choice but to continue to maintain good relations with Moscow, notwithstanding the difficulties that had begun to arise between the two countries.

Difficulties in Indo-Soviet relations

None the less, the relations between the two countries did not any more radiate the same warmth and the same level of friendliness as existed in the middle fifties. They were in fact seriously affected. The hitherto level of remarkable frankness and cordiality had become strikingly low; and the Soviet-Indian statements made in private meetings were now simple reiteration of what had been publicly stated. The Soviet attitude, for example, at the Indo-Soviet bilateral talks held in Delhi in 1968 was that of an imperial power dealing with a dependency. She did not even observe the elmentary diplomatic courtesies, as they brushed aside one Indian query after another, and studiously refused to offer satisfaction to the host country on any matter of direct concern to her. Whether the issue was the supply of Soviet arms to Pakistan or Moscow's neutralist stand on Kashmir, or the harsh and continuous propaganda that was beamed by *Radio Peace and Progress* against some of the Congress leaders. Even on the explosive issue of border alignment between India and China, shown on Soviet maps, the attitude of the Soviet delegation was generally evasive and non-committal. But the differences between the two countries were no more confined to a few political issues only. They had spilled over to the economic domain, where an increasing number of difficulties and differences had become evident.

On the question of trade, difficulties began to arise with the development of a favourable trade balance for India. This began in 1964 and reached the figure of 210 million rupees in 1967.[82] Such a trend is expected to continue in view of the fact that, having built an important industrial base, Indian needs for capital equipment have significantly declined, and

82. *Financial Times* (12 June 1968).

her demands for such commodities as fertilizers, industrial raw materials, non-ferrous metals etc. are rapidly rising.[83] The Soviet Union, which had so far met most of India's demands for capital equipment, is however unable to provide the new needs. None the less she appears to be insisting that India must buy from her in order to balance trade and payments between the two countries.

Difficulties also began to arise in some of the projects built by Moscow. Some of them were ill-equipped, while the others were in fields for which there did not appear to be much demand. For instance, the Indian Drugs and Pharmaceuticals Ltd. (IDIP) was dogged from the outset by faulty equipment, rising costs, designs unsuitable for Indian conditions, and delays in delivery. It was even suggested that much of the plant was in fact second-hand, having been built for China and dismantled. The Soviet project report had not included a feasibility study, estimates of demand having been assumed from Soviet experience elsewhere. Consequently, there was a heavy surplus at the plant. Indian consumption of the tetracycline group of drugs, for instance, was ten metric tons a year and was estimated to rise to 40-50 metric tons a year by 1971-72. But the Soviet experts none the less insisted on a capacity of 120 tons of chlorotetracycline, which had become obsolete and was not used by Indian doctors. The IDIP consequently incurred a loss of 8.9 million rupees in 1968.[84]

Difficulties were also discernible in the further development of the oil industry. After having acquired a dominant position in the Indian oil industry, Moscow was eager not to lose this position. The Soviet attitude to the exploring for oil in structures discovered off the Bombay coastline in the Gulf of Cambay is a case in point.[85] Preliminary investigations in 1963 indicated that these structures held promise of being some of the largest oil reserves in the world. It is interesting that

83. Indian imports of industrial raw materials between April and September 1968 were 40 per cent higher compared to the same period during 1967.
84. *Economic and Political Weekly* (5 October 1968).
85. *Thought* (14 September 1968) ; see also *Economic and Political Weekly* (7 September 1968).

Moscow admitted that its own expertise was inadequate to explore and develop the structures. But at the same time, it would not have other countries undertake the work, and has been pressurizing the Indian Government to go slow in the hope that it will be able to satisfy Indian technical needs within a few years.

The factor that perhaps contributed to the rise of most serious differences in Indo-Soviet relations was Moscow's reluctance to permit a large Indian participation in the implementation of Soviet-aided projects. The Soviet Government declined to share the construction of the Bokaro steel project with Indian consultants and forced on India 350 Soviet experts when the Indian Government was convinced that Indian engineers could do the job.[86] This was described by an observer as "an attempt to reduce us to that of contractor coolies".[87]

The Indian proposal for an economy of 20 billion rupees in a project of 90 billion was also rejected. Moscow very clearly informed New Delhi that either it could approve the project along with the original costs of production or alternatively drop it altogether. Furthermore, there have been four delays since the project was conceived in 1964 which have put the estimated completion date of the first stage to early 1973 compared with the original schedule of late 1968. These delays have pushed up the cost of the project over and over again to a fantastic figure. The Soviet consultants had originally undertaken to complete the first stage of the project at a cost of 5 billion and 900 million rupees. It is now likely to be around 8 billion rupees.[88]

In addition to all these difficulties, the over-all Soviet attitude towards India became increasingly difficult. More and more examples began to arise of Soviet annoyance with India, difficulties began to surge forward regarding the composition of delegations, criticism of internal Indian policies became more rampant in the Soviet press and anti-Indian

86. *The Statesman's Weekly* (14 May 1966).
87. *Ibid.*
88. *Economic Times* (4 February 1970).

propaganda—including personal attacks on some leaders—became common on *Radio Peace and Progress.*

Soviet ideological assessment of the Indian political and economic scene also underwent an important change by the middle sixties. While the *New Times* noted India's increasing dependence on United States aid and the "growing strength of the capitalist monopolies with the close foreign trade",[89] an article in *International Affairs* expressed the view that the control of the Indian big business was pushing her "off the path of independence".[90] Perhaps the most interesting analysis was by Professor R. Ulyanovsky, deputy head of the international department of the Soviet Central Committee. In an article in *Pravda* he rated India below the more recently independent countries in Africa in terms of revolutionary potential. The functioning of the state sector was considered to be far from promising in view of the fact that it was being "gradually converted into means of speeding up the development of privately owned industrial capitalism". The effect of this and other "retrograde" tendencies was, according to Ulyanovsky, to cancel out such favourable Indian features as "a progressive foreign policy" and "friendly relations with the Soviet camp".[91]

None the less, all these difficulties and irritations that are bound to surge forward even between any two friendly nations have not interfered with the basic Soviet desire to forge closer links with India. Apparently, the geopolitical and national interest considerations are the overriding factors that have tended to goad the Soviet leadership to continue to take positive steps to cultivate Indian friendship. Consider the whole range of Soviet policies during the Indo-Pakistan conflict of 1971. Notwithstanding the serious risks connected with the escalating dispute, a Treaty of Peace, Friendship and Cooperation was concluded with India, and open support was extended to that country during the entire period of the conflict.[92] India

89. *New Times* (11 August 1965).
90. *International Affairs* (April 1967).
91. *Pravda* (3 January 1969).
92. For different views on the treaty, see A. P. Jain, *Shadow of the Bear. The Indo-Soviet Treaty* (New Delhi : 1971).

obviously still remains an important factor in international affairs; and her large size, her relative political stability and reasonable economic growth cannot be ignored—least of all by the Soviet Union who is continuously seeking a viable counterbalance to the expanding Chinese influence on the continent of Asia.

Chapter IV

China and India

IF India and the Soviet Union have been continuously moving closer to each other, the relations between China and India, however, have witnessed the reverse process. Apart from a relatively short period of generalized euphoria when the two countries were quite close to each other, the relations—at least since 1958—slowly and steadily degenerated, reaching a snapping point with the explosion of the border conflict in 1962.

What are the reasons for such an evolution ? How come that the two most ancient civilizations of the world, whose long history of cultural relations has constituted "one of the central facts of Asian history",[1] have drifted into a situation of intense hostility ? How is it that, despite more than a century of common colonial experience during which the political leaders of both countries had often underlined their determination to develop meaningful relations, they have moved in the opposite direction after their political independence ? Is it in the nature of things that in the modern and contemporary periods of our history, where contact is greater, where ideologies are assertive, where economic expansiveness is rampant, varying degrees of conflict between neighbouring countries are unavoidable ?

All these and myriad other questions can be raised, the answers to which can be sought only through an analysis of the

1. K. M. Pannikar, *India and China . A Study of Cultural Relations* (Bombay : 1957), p. viii.

evolution of the relations between the two countries ; for one can, in this manner, effectively identify the various under-currents that determine different forms of inter-state relations.

The revolution of 1949 in China was undoubtedly a major development in the Asian sub-system. For the Chinese, this historic event projected forward a highly motivated political force which rapidly integrated a disunited country, expanded the infrastructure, restructured agriculture and developed some of the basic industries. For any developing country, the rapid introduction of these much-needed innovations would have had a major effect ; for uncertain, disunited and slumbering China it was simply dimensional.

However for non-Communist India, which was already wading through myriad internal difficulties, the dramatic events of 1949 in China were hardly a favourable sign ; for they had skewed the Asian balance of power in favour of the Communist world, which now was no longer a factor confined within the borders of the Soviet Union or that of a few countries of far away Europe, but had become a vital factor in the very heart of Asia. For those who subscribed to the Communist doctrine, it was naturally a favourable development which needed to be emulated by other countries, but for the Indian decision-makers who were denouncing and confronting the violent policies of the Communist Party of India it could hardly be characterized as an auspicious development. How could it be, when they, in co-operation with other Commonwealth countries, had decided in April 1950 to give co-ordinated joint aid to the Burmese Government to fight Communists, and when they avoided badgering the British to quit Malaya where the Communists dominated the nationalist movement ?

If the resurgence of Communist China in Asia was by no means a favourable development for India, the Communist occupation of Tibet was frankly disastrous ;[2] for it brought a new, dynamic and rather unfriendly state to the very doors of

2. A buffer zone was created in 1904 when the British Indian Government organized a military expedition against Tibet, with the fixed aim of "forestalling any likely collusion between the Dalai Lama and Russian agents". For details, see Alastair Lamb, *The China-India Border : The Origins of Disputed Boundaries* (London : 1964), pp. 142-147.

India. The buffer zone that the British had created and successfully maintained to protect the northern borders of British India now disappeared suddenly ; and for the first time the Himalayan region, which had hitherto remained dormant, suddenly became a live frontier generating a new strategic problem that India had never faced before. A new and unprecedented situation had thus developed on India's northern frontiers. Externally, she was now faced with a mighty coalition—China having accepted the Soviet evaluation of India —of two neighbours whose immense power and military strength were apparent, and whose attitude towards India was by no means friendly. The Chinese characterized India's policy of non-alignment as a camouflage, considered her still to be a semi-colony, and condemned Nehru as "an imperialist running dog belonging to the political garbage of India".[3] Mao Tse-tung personally went to the unusual lengths of cabling the full support of China to the Indian Communists in their violent struggle, and expressed the hope that the day was not far off when India would certainly not "remain long under the yoke of imperialism and its collaborators". "Like free China", he added, "a free India will one day emerge in the socialist and people's democratic family ; that day will end the imperialist reactionary rule in the history of mankind".[4]

The appearance of the new external threat, it is important to note, coincided with the weakening of India and the resurgence of a number of difficulties that she had not faced before. In the first place, the physical withdrawal of the British power left the country militarily weak. The strong protective hand of a major power was no longer there to pursue a forward—though undoubtedly imperialistic—policy to withstand effectively any attack from the north. Even the strongest viceroy, throughout the British period of Indian history, was not faced with the problem of having to deal with a united and well-organized China, or a militant Communist party within India, backed by powers across the Himalayas and the Pamirs.

Secondly, the partition of the sub-continent into two hostile

3. *World Culture* (22 July 1949).
4. For complete text of the letter, see V. B. Karnik (ed.), *Indian Communist Party Documents 1930-56* (Bombay : 1957), p. 48.

states, who did not wait long to head towards a collision course, rendered the nation weak, helpless and considerably preoccupied with defending her western frontiers. The striking example of this state of affairs was the remarkable inability of the Indian decision-makers to forestall Chinese occupation of Tibet—an area of vital importance to India. Only statements were made protesting against the violence of Chinese action and underlining the importance of peacefully resolving the Sino-Tibetan differences. In many ways, the Indian reaction was a striking example of the extent to which elements of continuity subsist in the foreign policy of a nation no matter who happens to be at the helm of affairs. The British, during the heydays of imperialism, had also responded in a similar manner, the only difference being that whereas they used their military power to implement their policies, the Indians appeared to have neither the determination nor the sinews of military strength to create an area of security around themselves.

The development of a threatening external situation none the less made it imperative for the Indian decision-makers to re-examine their foreign policy, to reassess the rapidly changing international situation, and to reformulate some of the essential tenets on which their foreign policy was based. Obviously they could no more bask in the glory of a moral stature they had developed for themselves, nor could they rely on their apparently ineffective military strength to face any threat that might emanate from nations that were bigger and stronger than their own.

But what could India do in the light of the new situation? The options were indeed limited and a leverage was almost non-existent in view of the well-defined bipolar situation. Considering the forthright decision of the Nehru Government to make non-alignment its article of faith, an alliance with the western world was hardly possible. Moreover, it was evident that such a decision would have only further exacerbated the tension and conflict in the area, making it even more difficult for the Indian leaders to surmount intractable problems facing the country.

However, if an open and a formal orientation in the direction of the West was difficult, an alliance with the Communist world was impossible, in view of the profound ideological and political gap that separated those who were in power in India from those who happened to be the decision-makers in Communist countries.

India's response to the threat

None the less, it was obvious that within the general conceptual framework of non-alignment, a new approach and some innovated thinking had become imperative to face the new situation. The monolithic unity of the two Communist giants was indeed too menacing to be ignored.

It was in response to this urgent need that a broad consensus emerged among the Indian decision-makers to deploy different efforts to face the new situation.

First of all a number of political and military steps were taken to strengthen India's defences. New treaties were negotiated with the vulnerable Himalayan States of Bhutan (1949), Sikkim (1950) and Nepal (1951), underlining in different degrees the interdependence between them and India. While in the case of Sikkim the protectorate status, existing already under the British, was continued,[5] the agreement with Bhutan provided that the Himalayan kingdom would be "guided by the advice of the Government of India in regard to its external relations".[6] With Nepal, however, only a treaty of "everlasting peace and friendship" was concluded.[7] But considering the strategic importance of the country, Nehru made it clear in a statement to the Indian Parliament that the Himalayas are mostly in the northern borders of India and "we cannot allow that barrier to be penetrated because it is the principal barrier of India. Therefore much as we appreciate the independence of Nepal, we cannot allow anything to go wrong in Nepal or permit that barrier to be crossed or weakened because that would be a risk to our own security".[8]

5. Government of India, *Foreign Policy of India, Texts of Documents* (New Delhi : 1958), p. 27.
6. Cited in Shanti Prasad Varma, *Struggle for the Himalayas : A Study in Sino-Indian Relations* (Delhi : 1965), p. 24.
7. Government of India, *op. cit.*, pp. 21-23.
8. Cited in P. C. Chakravarti, *India's China Policy* (Bloomington : 1962), pp. 43-44.

Discreet steps were also taken to improve communications throughout the mountainous tribal areas, to increase the number of checkposts in the middle sector, and to extend the rudiments of effective administration in the sensitive north-east frontier area right up to the McMahon line.[9] A high-level North and North-Eastern Border Defence Committee was established in 1952 to investigate the long-term aspects of Himalayan security and assess the requirements in the event of a clash with China.[10]

But most of these steps, it should be noted, were essentially diplomatic, police and administrative measures, the purpose of which was to bring about a modest improvement in India's defences. All concerted defence preparations were, however, studiously avoided either because of a fear of an adverse reaction from China or because of imperative economic needs which understandably had to be assigned top priority. One could also argue that the Indian decision-makers, who had hitherto devoted most of their political lives to non-violent action, perhaps did not have the perception—at least immediately after independence—to realize the danger of Chinese military action. In fact, within a few years after the independence of the country, the armed forces shrank rapidly in importance and national esteem even while Indian and Pakistani troops were confronting each other in Kashmir and elsewhere. The legacy of a potentially first-class army passed into the hands of a series of ministers of defence and commanders-in-chief of less than top quality.[11]

However, notwithstanding the partial strengthening of India's defences, there appeared to have emerged a clear consensus among the Indian leaders that political rapprochement with the Communist world was really the only rational substitute to a military confrontation ; for, in their view, there really did not seem to exist any other option that they could rationally decide for. Presumably India was too weak to defy any big nation,

9. See Lorne J. Kavic, *India's Quest for Security* (California : 1967), pp. 46-61.
10. Brigadier J. P. Dalvi (Retired), *Himalayan Blunder* (Bombay : 1969), p. 22.
11. For some details concerning Indian defence ministers, see S. S. Khera, *India's Defence Problem* (New Delhi : 1968), pp. 66-79.

and too concerned with playing a moral role in international affairs to jeopardize her position by having a showdown with any one of them.

It was in this frame of mind that a diplomatic offensive was launched to seek some normalization, if not complete understanding, with the Communist countries. China, being geographically and spiritually closer to India, naturally became the first objective of Indian diplomacy. Notwithstanding the radically different economic and political systems, the Indian leadership did not allow it to act as an obstacle to the development of cordial relations between the two countries. On the contrary, the emergence of a new and relatively stable China was formally looked upon favourably, and Nehru himself considered the developments in that country as a triumph of nationalism and as a clear sign of Asian regeneration. He was particularly anxious to avoid any action that might encourage the revolutionary, incredulous and highly motivated nation to isolate herself from the non-Communist world. Every effort, he argued, must therefore be made to encourage her to resume normal relations with other countries; for there was nothing, in his view, which brought out the belligerence in a nation than the absence of any contact with other countries.

Nehru therefore persistently argued that the development of friendly relations between Communist China and India was of vital importance to both countries. He demanded the admission of Peking into the United Nations, insisted on the return of Taiwan to the People's Republic, and declined to accept the invitation of the United States to go to San Francisco to sign the Japanese Peace Treaty on the ground that Communist China, one of the major victims of Japanese aggression during World War II, had refused to accept the American draft treaty. Furthermore, when China intervened in the Korean War, India refused to extend her support to the United Nations resolution which condemned Peking as an aggressor. In fact so great was Nehru's desire to seek understanding with China that even when Tibet—of vital importance to India—had been forcibly incorporated by Chinese troops in 1950, he avoided a showdown, though he did not fail to make it clear to Peking that his government did not approve such action.[12]

Twenty years after these events, Nehru's over-eagerness to seek an understanding with China is generally considered to have been an horrendous blunder. Considering all that has happened since then and the hindsight we have consequently developed, it is of course possible to be struck by his short-lightedness ; but it would have been certainly difficult to characterize it in such a manner in 1950 when the picture of the world was appreciably different. Communist China evidently was determined to integrate Tibet into the mainland, and there was not much that India could really do to forestall this tenacity of purpose—apart of course from making some political efforts that were in fact made in order to resolve the issue peacefully.

In many ways, one cannot escape the reflection that Nehru's objective of forging closer links with China was understandable. Her potential force and disconcerting proximity to India were too evident to be ignored—least of all by a country which had been divided and which was facing myriad internal and external problems. His perception, furthermore, of India's role in the world was such that it would have been seriously thwarted by the explosion of a serious conflict with Peking. However, where Nehru did prove short-sighted in 1950 was in his disinclination to increase effectively the sinews of India's military power to face the new and undoubtedly very complex situation. In any event, such a single-minded policy finally began to pay off ; for it became increasingly evident that Peking was slowly abandoning its belligerent line. The first signs of this change became apparent during the Korean War. The Chinese attitude underwent a change when it became apparent that Nehru's views on the conflict were by no means identical to those of the western countries. Chou En-lai paid tributes to him for his contribution to end the war,[13] and Mao Tse-tung, who personally proposed a toast at the first anniversary celebrations of the Indian Republic, spoke to the Indian Ambassador in warm

12. For the exchange of notes on Tibet, see International Commission of Jurists, *The Question of Tibet and the Rule of Law* (Geneva : 1959), pp. 132-138.

13. K. M. Pannikar, *In Two Chinas—Memoirs of a Diplomat* (London: 1955), p. 123.

terms about the Indian Prime Minister and expressed the hope of meeting him soon in China. He also underlined the importance of developing cultural and educational exchanges between the two countries.[14]

India's refusal to sign the Japanese Peace Treaty was also warmly received by the Chinese press. The *People's Daily* editorially welcomed India's decision to reject the San Francisco Treaty, and expressed the view that such an action proved "that age was past when imperialist governments can do whatever they please".[15] In another article, signed by a "political observer", on the same subject, the author went even further and characterized Indian action as "a development of utmost importance".[16] New Delhi was no longer considered tied to the apron strings of the West, and Nehru was no longer condemned as the "running dog of imperialism".

With great rapidity the relations between the two countries began to run on an even keel. Visits were exchanged, international affairs were amiably discussed, and a number of agreements were concluded, the most important of which was the agreement on Tibet (April 1954) containing the five principles of peaceful coexistence. It would be of course presumptuous to attribute the change in China's foreign policy exclusively to Indian patience and friendly initiatives. Obviously there was a host of different factors and circumstances that contributed to the formation of innovative policy. None the less, the Indian factor is important in so far as it was India's determination to adopt an independent attitude on many controversial issues directly concerning China that caused Chinese decision-makers to realize and appreciate the vital importance of non-alignment in international affairs.

Undoubtedly, this change was the major breakthrough for Indian diplomacy, for it disintegrated the monolithic view that the Communist world had developed of India, and inaugurated a new policy towards the non-Communist countries of Asia.

14. *Ibid.*
15. *People's China* (10 September 1951), p. 39.
16. *Ibid.*, p. 10.

Peaceful coexistence

The so-called period of peaceful coexistence was thus inaugurated.

Between June 1954 and January 1957, Chou En-lai paid five visits to India. On each occasion, he was given a warm welcome wherever he went. He held prolonged discussions with Nehru on international problems, reaffirmed his faith in Panch Sheela, and paid tributes to the host country for her "consistent and firm support" for the complete unification of the fatherland and admission to the United Nations.[17]

Nehru paid one visit to China in October 1954. He too was received with enthusiastic acclamation by the Chinese Government and people. In one of his speeches he emphasized the past friendship between the two countries. "The greatest need of the world today", he said, "is peace and I am convinced that the people of China like the people of India are devoted to the cause of peace. The joint statement issued by Chou En-lai and myself embodies the five principles which should govern the relationship between countries. These principles lay down the sovereign rule that each country should have freedom and independence and should live its own life in friendship with others but without any interference from outside."[18]

Supplementing these inter-governmental contacts, exchanges of other kinds were actively promoted. A 32-member Indian workers' delegation, for example, went to China in May 1955. This was followed in June 1955 by a cultural delegation, in September of the same year by a group of professors and students, and in July-September 1956 by a group of experts to study Chinese agrarian co-operatives. In return, Peking sent a number of delegations to India, the most important of which was the visit in 1955 of Soong Ching-ling, the Vice-Chairman of the Standing Committee of the National People's Congress.[19]

---

17. *Hindu* (1 December 1956).
18. *Keesing's Contemporary Archives* (1954), p. 13890.
19. For details, see Herbert Passin, *China's Cultural Diplomacy* (London : 1962) ; see also K. T. Shah, *The Promise that is New China* (Bombay : 1953) ; Raja Hutheesing, *Window on China* (London : 1953).

More important than these were the diplomatic and quasi-diplomatic gatherings in which the two countries participated. At the Geneva conference in 1954 a close co-operation was established between the two delegations. At the 11-nation non-official conference on relaxation of tension held in Delhi in 1955—at which China was present—a number of resolutions were adopted demanding *inter alia* the immediate lifting of embargo on trade with China and her admission to the United Nations. This was soon followed by the important 29-nation Afro-Asian Conference at Bandung which both Nehru and Chou En-lai attended along with premiers and foreign ministers of other participating governments. The cumulative effect of these continuous interchanges and co-ordinations on the cultural and diplomatic levels undoubtedly contributed to the general relaxation of tension. Myriad declarations underlined the historic friendship between the two countries ; and a number of books werepublished in which attempts were made to dig into the past of the two nations in order to discover the cultural links that may have existed in the remote past.

One often wonders whether this euphoric state of affairs did not contribute to the diminution of the Indian capacity of rationally assessing the development of a threat from the north. It is indeed an open question, the answer to which may be found in the still unavailable archival material.

In any event, one thing is certain, the Chinese decision-makers did not appear to be carried away by the euphoria of Sino-Indian relations. They did not appear to have lost sight of their national interest, of the vital necessity of soberly examining the over-all situation in the area, of seeking other allies, and of neutralizing potential enemies. India was undoubtedly an important factor in Chinese diplomatic calculations, but there were other nations whose importance to China was by no means underestimated.

Peking's relations with Pakistan is a case in point. Despite the latter's decision to join the Southeast Asia Treaty Organization (SEATO) and the Baghdad pact, China took steps to forge closer links with her.[20] Although Peking's official reaction

---

20. For some details, see H. Kapur, "China's Relations with India and Pakistan", *Current History* (September 1969).

was obviously critical of Pakistan's decision to hinge her fate on the West, it was none the less in sharp contrast to the vitriolic outburst from Moscow. In fact, the Chinese Government did not send any protest to Karachi, and Pakistan was not singled out for derogatory comments by the Chinese leaders and newspapers. At the Bandung conference (1955), the Chinese Premier actually went to the extent of accepting Pakistan's Prime Minister Mohammad Ali's assurances that his country would not be involved in any conflict that might be unleashed by the United States against China. Trade was increased and an increasing number of cultural delegations were exchanged. The 12-day visit to China of the Pakistani Prime Minister, H. S. Suhrawardy, in October 1956 was made an important occasion for giving him a tremendous ovation.[21] The joint communique that was issued at the end of the visit recognized "the need for the development of commercial and cultural relations" and recorded the fact that "there is no conflict of interests between the two countries".[22]

Why did China adopt a remarkably sober and moderate attitude ? Why did the Chinese accept Pakistan's assurances ? First of all, the Chinese knew that Pakistan had joined SEATO not because she had any special reason to fear Chinese Communism, or because she had any serious difficulties with Peking. For the Pakistani decision-makers, the increasing differences with India were far more important and far more real than the relatively non-existent danger of Communism; and the potential danger of military complications with India appeared to be more real than complications with China or the Soviet Union.

Secondly, the Chinese were probably aware that Pakistan was not too deeply involved in the defence arrangements contemplated under SEATO. With the exception of the modest role of the Pakistani navy, no Pakistani troops had participated in SEATO military exercises in spite of the fact that Pakistan maintained a larger defence establishment than either the Philippines or Thailand.

21. For details, see B. L. Sharma, *The Pakistan-China Axis* (Bombay : 1968).
22. K. Sarwar Hasan, *op. cit.*, p. 363.

It is therefore not surprising that China decided to maintain a measure of flexibility in her relations with Pakistan. This was especially evident in her stand on Kashmir. While privately assuring India that she understood and appreciated the Indian position on the Kashmir issue, she publicly abstained from supporting one side against the other, and expressed the hope that the two countries would settle the issue peacefully.

Development of Sino-Indian conflict

The euphoric state of Sino-Indian relations, however, did not last too long, as a number of political developments contributed to the degeneration of the over-all situation and the inauguration of the period of confrontation between the two countries. Internally the gradualist and moderate approach, characterized by the "blooming and contending" movement, was abruptly ended in 1958. A vigorous programme of political education was initiated to eradicate "erroneous" thoughts that were increasingly on the ascendant among Chinese intellectuals. In the economic field, the policy of the "great leap forward" was inaugurated with considerable fanfare.[23]

Externally, considerable stress was now laid on the decisive tilting of the international balance in favour of the socialist countries as a result of the launching of the intercontinental ballistic missile in August 1957, on the unchanging character of American policy to dominate the world, and on the insensate policy of extending unconditional Communist support to the nationalists in the third world countries who, "in the final analysis", cannot "escape the clutches of control of imperialism".[24]

Within the general framework of the new militant posture, India unavoidably became the principal target of Chinese hostility. A number of Indian political parties were accused of fomenting the Tibetan revolt of March 1959, and the Indian Parliament was denounced for interfering in the internal affairs of China. An unusually long editorial appeared in the *People's Daily* on 6 May in which, alternating between condescending friendliness and outspoken intransigence, Nehru was criticised

23. *Supra* Chapter II.
24. Wang Cheo-Hsiang, *op. cit.*

for his views on Tibet. For the first time (January 1959) the entire border alignment between India and China was questioned, and in September of the same year, after a series of escalating border incidents, a formal claim was laid to about 50,000 square miles of what the Indians considered to be a part of their territory.

Nothing would, of course, be more simplistic than to attribute the open manifestation of these differences exclusively to the left-wing orientation of Chinese politics. And nothing would be more undiscerning and more aberrant than to suggest that the Chinese were raising illusory and non-existing issues ; for differences and difficulties had existed before. Consider the myriad letters, notes and memoranda etc. exchanged in the mid-fifties, in which the differences between New Delhi and Peking had clearly been established on the question of boundary alignment. Sometimes the correspondence was pertaining to a pass in the western sector and sometimes it was concerned with the border in the eastern sector.[25]

All this had thus existed before 1958 and was by no means an artificial creation of the Chinese leaders. But, during the period of peaceful coexistence, when they were seeking a common ground with India, they considered it expedient to remain relatively uncommunicative on issues that divided the two nations. During 1958-59, when signs of belligerence and radicalism were becoming increasingly evident, when China was convinced of Indian "complicity" in the Tibetan revolt, and when her military presence on the border had been sufficiently reinforced, the differences with India were allowed to bubble to the surface.

But the differences with India were not an exception. They were a syndrome of a series of tensions that were rapidly building up with a number of countries in the Asian sub-system. Difficulties were surging forward with a number of non-aligned countries, and with some of them they appeared to have reached a snapping point. With the Soviet Union serious signs of rising tension and differences were becoming

25. For details, see Ministry of External Affairs, *Notes, Memoranda and Letters Exchanged and Agreements Signed between the Governments of India and China 1954-1959* (New Delhi : 1963).

evident. With the United States difficulties appeared to have reached a point of no return after the explosion of the Taiwan crisis in 1958.[26]

All these developments naturally placed China in a state of serious isolation. For she was now estranged not only from her friends but also from her allies. The development of such a difficult situation would be considered as serious for any country. For developing China, faced with serious internal problems, it was disastrous, since she had neither the military power nor the economic strength to stand on her own feet— an essential pre-condition for any nation that wishes to pursue an independent and defiant policy.

China turns to the third world

Thus by any standards, China's foreign policy was signally unsuccessful in 1958 ; and it was evident that a re-examination of her strategy and tactics had become more than necessary in order to break out of the uncomfortable and increasingly dangerous encirclement.

But what could China do to make the situation less un-favourable ? How could she face internal difficulties and neutralize any external danger without of course openly sacri-ficing some of her basic principles ? An understanding with the United States or the Soviet Union was considered impossible ; for any concession to either of them would have involved, in Chinese perception, a basic retreat on fundamental issues.

If the scope of an understanding with the two super-powers appeared limited, a conciliation and rapprochement with the third world countries was now considered possible. For by forging closer ties with these countries, she might be able to mobilize the power of these nations to establish moral restraints against the super-powers.[27]

Within the framework of this general interest in the third world, an effort was made to seek some understanding with India. After a series of border incidents had mounted tension between the two countries, Chou En-lai, in a letter dated 7'

26. *Supra*, Chapter II.
27. *Supra*, Chapter II.

November 1959, proposed to Nehru that "the Prime Ministers of the two countries hold talks in the immediate future".[28] It was obvious that no talks could be held as long as the border clashes continued. To ensure border tranquillity during the period of negotiations, he proposed "that the armed forces of China and India each withdraw 20 kilometres at once from the so-called McMahon line in the East, and from the line up to which each side exercises actual control in the West, and that the two sides undertake to refrain from again sending their armed personnel to be stationed in and patrol the zone from which they have evacuated their armed forces".[29] In order to counter the expected Indian objection that such a withdrawal would permit the Chinese still to remain deeply entrenched within Indian territory, he clearly stated that his government was prepared to consider a further withdrawal "if there is need to increase the distance".[30]

It was not easy for Nehru to accept either the proposal for an immediate meeting or the suggested interim measures for border pacification. Public opinion was too enraged, and many leading members of the government were too committed to the objective of obtaining a Chinese withdrawal from the recently occupied territory to permit him to accept the Chinese proposals. He therefore made counter-proposals. In the north-east, he suggested that the McMahon line should remain the frontier, and that there should not be the slightest risk of any border clash if each government would instruct its outposts not to send out patrols. As regards Longju, he proposed that China should withdraw, and India, in return, would not reoccupy. In regard to the Ladakh area, the Indian Prime Minister offered to withdraw all his personnel to the west of the line shown as the international boundary in the Chinese map of 1956, provided China on her part would similarly withdraw all the personnel to the east of the international boundary as shown in Indian official maps and described in Indian notes.[31]

28. Foreign Languages Press, *Sino-Indian Border Question* (Peking : 1960), p. 17.
29. *Ibid.*, p. 16.
30. *Ibid.*
31. Government of India, *White Paper* No. III (New Delhi : 1960), pp. 46-50.

In his letter of 17 December, Chou En-lai rejected Nehru's proposal on the ground that such a proposal would have meant Chinese withdrawal from 20,000 square miles—including the Aksai Chin area, over which they had constructed a vital road linking Sinkiang with Tibet.[32] In contrast, this would have involved Indian evacuation of only one post, Demchok, in the extreme south-east of the disputed area and perhaps 50 square miles around.[33] The Chinese Prime Minister repeated his plea for a summit meeting "so as to reach first some agreement on principles as a guidance to concrete discussions and settlement of the boundary question by the two sides".[34] To clinch the issue further, he suggested December 26 as the date on which he and Nehru should meet either in China or in Rangoon.[35] Nehru again refused the proposal on the ground that they could not reach agreement on principles "when there is such complete disagreement about the facts".[36] On this he appeared adamant.

Sino-Indian talks

However, hardly three weeks had gone by when the Indian public was startled by the news that the Indian Prime Minister had suddenly invited Chou En-lai to a bilateral meeting in New Delhi.

What led to this unexpected shift in Indian policy? Why did Nehru suddenly agree to meet Chou En-lai when he had so firmly resisted all such proposals? Although the exact reasons are obviously not known, one can assume that the Soviet Union must have exercised considerable pressure to bring about a change in the Indian attitude. This state of affairs hardly left any choice to the Nehru Government ; for, faced with an aggravating dispute, it could hardly afford to antagonize the Soviet Union, as any development of such a nature would have negated the Indian policy of non-alignment, and would have led the Indian decision-makers once again to turn to the West. Fur-

32. *Ibid.*, pp. 51-55.
33. Neville Maxwell, *India's China War* (London : 1970), p. 138.
34. *White Paper* No. III, p. 55.
35. *Ibid.*
36. *Ibid.*, p. 56.

thermore, the categorical refusal by Nehru to meet Chou En-lai, unless certain conditions were met, was by no means a popular stand in the eyes of many nations, least of all on the part of a nation who had continuously harped on the vital importance of negotiations to resolve intractable international issues. In fact, Peking appeared to have already begun to make propaganda capital among the Communist and non-aligned nations by underlining the importance of peace and by stressing the unreasonableness of India.

However, in the prevailing state of public opinion, which already appeared bemused and enraged at the sudden extension of an invitation to Chou En-lai,[37] it was not possible for Nehru to conduct negotiations on a give-and-take basis. The political atmosphere was too charged and public opinion was too entrenched in a rigid position to permit the government to open any meaningful negotiations to break the seemingly intractable deadlock. In fact the Indian Prime Minister had considerably narrowed his own options and deprived himself of all room for manoeuvre by openly suggesting on a number of occasions that his coming meeting with Chou En-lai would not be "negotiations" but only "talks".

Therefore, when Chou En-lai, during his visit to New Delhi in April 1960, proposed the interesting and perhaps not too unreasonable bargain of dropping the Indian claim over Aksai Chin in lieu of a formal Chinese recognition of the McMahon line, it was rejected. The negotiations failed, though the two Prime Ministers agreed that the officials of the two governments should meet to examine all relevant documents in support of the stands of the two governments, and report. The Chinese Prime Minister went back from the Indian capital disappointed, embittered and in an unusual rage—to which he gave vent at a press conference in Khatmandu where he flew from New Delhi.

Sino-Indian conflict

India's rejection of Chou's proposal was taken by Peking as a signal for tougher action and it was probably this which led

---

37. On 16 February, the Opposition tabled an adjournment on the Government's "sudden and unwarranted reversal" of policy.

the Chinese leaders to precipitate a showdown with India. The border incidents between the two countries now became more frequent and verbal attacks more vitriolic. Nehru began to compare Chinese actions on the border "to the atrocities of Hitler in the modern age,"[38] and the Chinese openly identified Nehru with the "expansionist philosophy of the Indian big bourgeoisie".[39]

But what was perhaps even more serious was the decision of the Nehru Government to pursue a "forward policy" by which Indian army patrols were to be sent into the Chinese-occupied Aksai Chin area from the beginning of 1960 to establish an Indian presence by the interposition of Indian posts and patrols between Chinese positions. To the professional generals of the Indian Army, who were obviously familiar with conspicuous weaknesses in the Indian armour, this forward policy seemed exceedingly hazardous.[40] At both the western and eastern ends of the disputed boundary, the Chinese had established feeder roads that brought truck supplies and reinforcements to their front-line posts. The Indian army, on the other hand, had no roads anywhere near the forward positions. All supplies, even sometimes water, had to come by airdrop. Troops patrolling at 14 or 15 thousand feet had to be acclimatized to the difficult conditions, and frontier patrols often went forward with only the ammunition and blankets they could carry on their backs. In the face of these logistic and climatic difficulties, the Indian Army leaders resisted carrying out these obviously difficult assignments. But this was not for long, for political generals, who had not displayed any striking military competence, were placed in high positions in 1961 with the specific purpose of carrying out a wholly unrealistic policy which did not correspond to the real military strength.

What were the reasons that led Nehru to take such a calculated risk ? Why did he believe that the Chinese would not respond forthwith to any limited Indian military action ?

38. Jawaharlal Nehru, *Prime Minister on Sino-Indian Relations* (New Delhi : 1962).

39. *More on Nehru's Philosophy in the Light of Sino-Indian Boundary Question* (Peking : 1962).

40. For details, see Brigadier J. P. Dalvi (Retired), *op. cit.*, pp. 66-75.

While it would, of course, be difficult to give an assertive answer as long as diplomatic papers of the period are not accessible, one could venture to suggest that part of the answer to this puzzling conundrum perhaps lies in the internal as well as the international situations. During the period in question, China was facing myriad difficulties. Internally the country was slowly recovering from the dangerous after-effects of the great leap forward. The economy appeared dislocated, and a number of signs were clearly evident of rampant factionalism within the upper echelons of the party leadership. Externally China was increasingly becoming isolated. Tension was still mounting with the United States and increasing difficulties with the Soviet Union had already bubbled to the surface. Such a situation may have led the Indian decision-makers to conclude that China might be sluggish and prudent to some of their military initiatives.[41]

But the Indian evaluation was obviously based on a serious miscalculation; for in the face of the Indian forward policy, the Chinese violently reacted by a massive and surprisingly rapid attack on Indian positions, leading to the serious defeat of Indian troops in the bordering areas.[42] But this was not a simple military defeat. It was a defeat of all of India's ideals and a brutal exposure of her weaknesses and of her obvious inability to defend her interests and her security. For the first time it really dawned on the Indians that despite their moral stature, despite their generally acceptable role in international affairs, they were unable to withstand an attack from the outside and that they felt obliged to seek assistance from nations whom they did not consider as their close friends. This was indeed a very serious crisis—a crisis which had undermined India's policy of non-alignment.

However, this was not all. There were other striking examples of set-backs. Nepal, on whom India had hitherto exercised significant influence and for whose independence she had played a meaningful role, could no longer be considered as a close ally and friend ; for the powerful Chinese presence on her northern

41. Néville Maxwell, *op. cit.*, p. 225.
42. For details about the war, see Brigadier J. P. Dalvi, *op. cit.* ; see also Lt. General B. M. Kaul, *The Untold Story* (New Delhi : 1967).

borders had forced her to adopt posture of neutrality in the Sino-Indian conflict—a posture India had preached to the outside world since independence. Indian influence over Bhutan and Sikkim had become increasingly hazardous. Both the Himalayan kingdoms had become victims of Chinese intrigues and in one of them an effort allegedly was made to dethrone those elements that were known to be pro-Indian. For how long could these small and very vulnerable countries withstand pressure from the north ? Would they not, in due course, also adopt a posture of neutrality in order to maintain their position ? Is not the recent admission of Sikkim to the United Nations an indication of this trend ? At present we can perhaps assert with confidence that this will not happen. But can such an affirmative assertion be given for the future—especially when it is becoming increasingly evident that China has effectively stabilized her position in neighbouring Tibet ? Relations with neighbouring Burma and Ceylon were also no longer very cordial. Burma, who has always been suspicious of India, had displayed no hesitation—with India watching helplessly—in confiscating property of Indian nationals; and Ceylon placed in cold storage the agreement that was concluded with the Shastri Government concerning the future of Indians in Ceylon.

Indian reaction to defeat

The general plummeting of India's prestige and influence was indeed a great eye-opener ; for it generated a consensus in favour of fundamentally re-examining her role and her objectives in international affairs : was the general objective of acquiring a moral stature in the world really that important ? Was real and viable influence in international affairs determined by moral principles or was it the result of the quantum of military and economic power that a nation possessed ? Was it more vital and more urgent to resolve the problems of other nations than one's own ? Was it in the interest of the nation to assign the responsibility of formulating and conducting foreign policy to a few esoteric individuals or should it be the product of a general consensus openly arrived at after considerable debate and discussion ? All these and many other issues pertaining to foreign relations were extensively discussed in the country.

Looking at the India of 1963-64, it seemed as if this discussion was going to introduce a major dichotomization in the politics of the nation, and as if this collective and disorganized wandering over the entire range of difficult and explosive problems was going to generate even greater bemusement in the country. But this, happily, was not the case ; for slowly a concordance appears to have emerged. It was generally agreed that India must turn inwards, that she must concentrate on vital problems she was faced with nearer home, that she must realize the effectiveness of force in international affairs, and that foreign policy could no more be considered the exclusive domain of a few people.

Such consensus and thinking were partly, as stated above, the result of the 1962 debacle. But this was not the only reason. The disappearance of Nehru, and the rapidly changing political situation, were the other contributory factors. The political situation had become increasingly uncertain, regional forces had become more assertive, and the political parties had become more vigilant and more demanding. The death of Nehru further aggravated the political atmosphere in the country. It created a serious vacuum in political leadership. Those who successively succeeded him were apparently not of the same mettle. They neither possessed his dimensional approach to international affairs, nor did they have the charisma that surrounded his personality. In many ways this was what India needed ; for the new leaders who were projected on the Indian scene took a practical view of the world, and avoided—probably for the sake of their own political survival—taking any diplomatic initiatives that would take them away from the general consensus that appeared to have emerged.

One of the first issues to which considerable attention was therefore given by the Indian decision-makers was to strengthen the defences of the country. A blueprint for expansion was sanctioned including the creation of a modernized and well-equipped army of 825,000 men, the construction and improvement of communications, the stabilization of the Air Force at 45 squadrons.[43] Military assistance from friendly nations was

43. For details, see L. J. Kavic, op. cit. ; see also S. S. Khera, op. cit.

freely accepted,[44] and there was now a growing awareness of the feelings and the needs of the Indian armed forces. Even the question of acquiring nuclear weapons was publicly broached[45] and the Indian decision-makers—unlike in the past—appeared to wish to keep their options open.[46]

But all these developments were by no means a match for China's military superiority, though they are probably adequate in a limited conflict confined to the Sino-Indian border. In addition to a well-disciplined professional army of about 2.9 million strong, a large people's militia was formed in China. Important strides were also made in the nuclear field in the mid-sixties, when a series of nuclear and thermonuclear explosions was effectuated. That China had made remarkable progress in this field was evident from the fact that the last few tests involved a fusion (thermonuclear) device with a yield of some 3 megatons.[47] In the missile delivery system too, Peking appears to have made the great leap forward. In fact, about 20 medium-range missiles have already been deployed[48] and, according to all indications, they have overcome all the obstacles in the development of inter-continental ballistic missiles.[49]

Therefore, notwithstanding the remarkable improvement in India's defences, it is indeed questionable whether she would be able effectively and independently to withstand a significant military showdown with China. Even if she were to acquire a small nuclear arsenal, it is evident that it could not serve as an effective deterrent as long as she has not clearly opted for a prohibitively expensive, sophisticated delivery system capable of

44. The Indian leaders no longer considered military aid as incompatible with non-alignment. This was evident even before. See Nehru's statement cited in *The Times* (12 November 1962).

45. For details, see Major-General D. Som Dutt, *India and the Bomb. Adelphi Papers*, No. 30 (London, Institute of Strategic Studies : 1966) ; see also Institute for Defence Studies and Analyses, *A Strategy for India for a Credible Posture against a Nuclear Adversary* (New Delhi : 1968).

46. *Christian Science Monitor* (Boston : 28 July 1970).

47. *The Military Balance 1971-1972* (London : 1971), pp 40-42.

48. *Ibid* , p. 40.

49. *International Herald Tribune* (Paris : 21-22 February 1970).

reaching the Chinese industrial-military complex located far away from the Indian border.   The steel plants at Anshan, for example, are 2200 miles away, Mukden 2500, Shanghai 2150, Hankow 1750 and Chungking 1300.   The task of covering such distances without a sophisticated delivery system is therefore not an easy one,[50] whereas India's major cities and industrial complexes are acutely vulnerable even to conventional air power based in Tibet.

This military imbalance between the two nations has not failed to affect the Indian situation. In the first place, it has generated a feeling of insecurity that was hitherto undiscernible in India's perception of the outside world. Secondly, the military imbalance has considerably diminished the significant leverage that she once had over a number of small neighbouring countries. No longer is she immune from an attack, and no longer is it possible to ignore the major problems of defence as she had often done during the heydays of India's great role in international affairs.   No longer do neighbouring small nations turn to India for help and guidance as it was often the case in the past, and no more are they prepared to underline with alacrity the great cultural ties that have united them with India. The power that grows out of the barrel of the Chinese gun being infinitely stronger than that of India has encouraged some of them to adopt a disengaged attitude towards India.

In the face of such a situation what can India do ? How can she enhance her security ? What can she do to neutralize any threat that she may perceive from China ?

While continuing further to improve her defences, the obvious and probably the most appropriate solution to such a problem would be the slow and steady normalization of relations between the two countries. This could be slowly achieved by initiating small steps that would generate a climate of confidence, which is most essential before broaching some of the intractable issues that have separated the two nations.

Alternatively, if this should prove difficult, which seems to be the case, the very nature of Indian insecurity may drive her to pursue a politics of alliances with nations who can give her the necessary protection.

50. Major-General D. Som Dutt, *op. cit.*, p. 6.

Conclusions

ONE of the most striking developments since World War II has been the remarkable resurgence of the third world in the international system. Within a brief span of about two decades almost all the nations hitherto subjected to protracted political domination by the colonial powers have become independent. While some of them had gained their political independence after a long and difficult period of continuous struggle, the others had become politically sovereign through a process which was relatively short and peaceful.

Obviously, there was a wide spectrum of politico-economic factors that had contributed to the ushering in of this historic process. There was the apparent inability of the colonial powers—rendered weak by World War II—to flourish their imperial might. There were the stresses and strains of Japanese occupation of Southeast Asia that contributed to the promotion of nationalism among many countries; and there was the continual international pressure on the colonial powers to unconsolidate their hold on the colonies.[1] But the most important factor that led to the disintegration of colonialism, however, was the rapid escalation of nationalist movements in many countries of Africa and Asia. In one country after the other, the basis of resistance to the foreign colonial power was

---

1. For background information on nationalism in the developing countries, see Rupert Emerson, *From Empire to Nation* (Boston : 1966).

increasingly broadened, and the links between the leaders and the people were meaningfully forged.[2]

That this historic development has radically transformed the international society is evident from the fact that the newly independent nations—along with convulsive Latin America—now have a significant voice on many issues that face the international community. In fact the quantum of nations belonging to this area now constitutes a majority in the international system. Admittedly, all of them are poor and have still a long and difficult road to traverse before acquiring—if ever—the sinews of economic and military power needed to influence world decisions, admittedly the quantitative predominance is by no means the principal determinant of the present and future trends of the international system. Even a cursory glance at the recent evolution of international relations would undoubtedly show the existence of a significant linkage between power and international decision-making, between power and the capacity of a nation to defy diverse international pressures.

None the less, considering the fact that the whole shape of contemporary international relations is being increasingly determined by the relatively new idea of sovereign equality,[3] the role of the third world countries is by no means insignificant. The explosive political forces surging forward in many countries of the area are in the process of changing the whole balance of power in the world, even though their economic and military power are negligible in the global system, and even though the political life of many of them may remain convulsive for years to come.[4]

If the role of the third world has become significant in the international system, the quantum of political, economic and revolutionary activities that one is continuously witnessing in these areas is even more striking. Consider the myriad revolutionary

2. For an interesting interpretation of the evolution of nationalism, see Geoffrey Barraclough, *An Introduction to Contemporary History* (London : 1967).

3. For details concerning this problem see Robert Klein, *The Idea of Equality in International Politics* (Geneva : 1966).

4. For background information on the potential role of developing countries, see E.F. Penrose, *The Revolution in International Relations* (London : 1965).

movements that have resurged forward in these areas. Consider the number of *coups d'etat* and the limited wars that many of them have painfully experienced, and consider the general economic and political upheavals that they are continuously subjected to.

Europe, which, until about two decades ago, was the "critical zone of the world" from where most of the global decisions had originated, had considerably declined in status and influence.[5] It has now settled down to a period of stability, and intense activity of calm and calculated negotiations in order peacefully to decide some of the residual problems with which it is still faced.

It is evident that no nation could afford to ignore this historic development—least of all the two highly motivated Communist giants, the Soviet Union and China, who, like the United States, considered their own vital interests inextricably linked with the international environment.

Consequently, many of the third world countries became important targets of intense Soviet and Chinese actions.[6] Sometimes, as we have seen in the preceding chapters, the tactics deployed towards these nations were of a revolutionary nature, while there were other occasions when it was considered more appropriate and more effective to limit their actions principally to inter-state activity.

There were also, however, other periods in the contemporary histories of the two nations when both the policies were perceptible in many of their actions. Very often this particular situation, where contradictory policies were collaterally pursued, was a sign of differences within the power structure of that nation. Behind the facade of monolithic unity, there were presumably diverse forces with variant perceptions pulling the nation in different directions.

In any event, one thing is certain : notwithstanding the wide spectrum of activities that was discernible in the external

5. Raymond Aron, "L'Histoire universelle se deplace vers l'orient", *Le Figaro* (7 October 1971).
6. For background information on the policies of the two countries, see Brian Crozier, *The Struggle for the Third World* (London : 1966).

behaviours of the two Communist giants, they did not pursue dissimilar policies during the initial stages of the Sino-Soviet friendship. Their revolutionary perceptions appeared to be more or less the same, and their national interests—though by no means identical—did not seriously collide.

But all this did not last long. For by the early sixties different attitudes and perceptions between the two nations became increasingly discernible. At first, while ignoring each other, while avoiding a conflict, they adopted different policies. But, soon, both of them began unavoidably to head towards a collision course openly undermining the influence of the other. Everywhere, this exacerbation was becoming increasingly evident, and almost everywhere no stone was left unturned to isolate and openly denigrate each other. While the Soviet Union was making efforts to maintain her economic and political hold on Eastern Europe, China was encouraging independent Communist forces to surge forward and defy the Soviet influence. While the Soviet Union was striving to stymie the political and economic unification of Western Europe, the Chinese appeared to be subtly encouraging this trend.

In the third world too, such a trend was clearly discernible. In one area after the other, there was a systematic determination on the part of both the countries to use all political, diplomatic, ideological and economic weapons available in their armours to undermine each other. If one of them projected a revolutionary image, the other sought to neutralize it by formulating even more revolutionary goals. If one succeeded in gaining some diplomatic influence in a country, the other openly sought friendship or alliance with some other nation in the area to destroy this influence. The two Communist giants thus had moved from one extreme position to the other—from great friendship to intense enmity. It is in the nature of almost all inter-state conflicts that they invariably culminate in a search for friends or allies in order to strengthen their own position *vis-a-vis* the enemy. Even a cursory reading of the diplomatic history of the preceding periods would clearly show the rampant prevalence of such a phenomenon Curiously enough, this continual search for alliances was not only made by nations who were militarily vulnerable to the attacks of the enemy, but was also pursued by nations whose military might was unchallengable, and who did not really need any ally in order to withstand any external attack or pressure. Presumably such a continual and persistent pursuit by almost all the nations in conflict—regardless of their needs—can be attributed to the political and psychological desire of avoiding a state of isolation in the international system; for isolation in a world which is increasingly becoming smaller is generally considered to be the most striking example of failure in the foreign policy of a nation.

The Sino-Soviet dispute is by no means an exception to this basic rule of international relations. Notwithstanding their assertion that traditional rules of behaviour are irrelevant to the relations between socialist states, one discerns almost the same phenomena, the same reaction and the same mode of behaviour as are generally found to exist among the non-socialist states.

In this struggle for influence, one of the areas to which the two Communist giants turned was the Indian sub-continent. That it was this area which became the principal target of Sino-Soviet dispute is understandable ; for it was this area which, because of its favourable strategic location, its relatively developed infrastructure and its large size, was perceived to have a potentially significant bearing on the general orientation of the Asian sub-system.

First of all, an effort was made by China and the Soviet Union to concentrate on India. Her large size, vast population, developed Communist party and a viable political structure were viewed as decisive factors in the tilting of the political balance. An Indian orientation in the direction of Moscow— apart from numerous political advantages—would have simultaneously exposed China's vast borders in the north as well as in the south; whereas the Indian decision to turn to Peking would not only have secured an element of stability on the Sino-Indian border, but would have considerably limited the scope of Soviet political influence in Southeast Asia and in some of the other areas of the third world.

China was in a disadvantageous position in this competitive battle ; for the increasingly intractable border dispute with India made it impossible for the two nations to reach any solid, viable and lasting understanding. In fact, the imperatives of conflicting national interests caused them to drift apart, and led to such exacerbation and to such heights of mutual recrimination that any hope of even a normalization of relations appeared to be forlorn.

The Soviet Union, on the other hand, was remarkably successful in forging close ties with India. The absence of a common border is, more often than not, an advantage as it conveniently removes one major issue from the list of problems that have invariably contributed to inter-state conflicts throughout history. Therefore subtly, and carefully avoiding any other controversial issues that might have inhibited the development of good relations, a systematic campaign was launched to help India economically and militarily and to solicit Indian support on myriad international issues. It is interesting to note that the remarkably sophisticated and calculated policy—developed recently after considerable effort—of a balanced approach towards India and Pakistan was cast to the winds and open support was extended to India. A treaty of "peace, friendship and co-operation" was suddenly concluded after two long years of negotiations,[7] and open support was extended to India in the Indo-Pakistan dispute of December 1971. All the resolutions unfavourable to India that were proposed to the Security Council of the United Nations were blocked, and all the great powers, including China, were warned to keep out of the Indo-Pakistan war from which India was emerging victorious.

Peking thus was faced with a very difficult situation. Instead of finding reliable allies and friends against a possible Soviet threat, it was now faced with the hazardous task of confronting a collateral danger from the south. Admittedly, the Indian threat was by no means as great and as perilous as the one from the Soviet side. Admittedly, the sinews of Chinese military and political power were far greater than that of their southern neighbour. However, if the danger from India alone was only marginal, it was evident that it could acquire a staggering dimension when closely co-ordinated with the Soviet Union.

What could the Chinese decision-makers do to face effec-

7. For full text, see *Soviet News* (10 August 1971).

tively the new situation ? How could they neutralize a simul-
taneous attack on two large fronts by two big nations and face,
at the same time, an American presence on their periphery ?

It is evident that all these questions, undoubtedly very intractable, must have been broached within the Chinese hierarchy
already in the late fifties ; for the shape of Indo-Soviet relations
was already becoming quite clear at that time. However, the
difficult circumstances existing in the aftermath of the great leap
forward made it difficult for the Chinese leaders to seek a
global response to the new development. The over-all Chinese
perception of the world was still too ideologically oriented,
and inflexibility in foreign policy was still too rampant, to permit
them to make major moves to counteract a situation which was
increasingly becoming unfavourable. However, if a major and
general initiative still appeared impossible, a flexible and non-
ideological move was none the less made towards Pakistan.

The rising Soviet influence in India and the growing Indian
consensus to opt for viable and meaningful understanding with
Moscow led the Chinese decision-makers to develop close and
firm ties with Pakistan. For by so doing, they considered that
they could, on the one hand, keep India preoccupied with the
situation in the area, and, on the other, deny to Moscow the
possibility of exercising preponderant influence on the whole
sub-continent. It is indeed striking that, notwithstanding the
fact that the Cultural Revolution made it generally impossible
to deal with these staggering issues with any flexibility, the
Chinese decision-makers continued to develop close and friendly
relations with Pakistan.

That such a policy was partially successful is evident from
the fact that India remained preoccupied with the situation on
the sub-continent, and was, at the same time, restrained from
giving a decisive blow to vulnerable Pakistan. However, the
success of such a policy was not only due to Chinese determination to come to the rescue of Pakistan—though this was not
unimportant—but was also due to the absence of any apparent
Soviet determination to deter China from interfering in the
Indo-Pakistan conflict. Consider the Indo-Pakistan war of
1965. The Chinese factor was undoubtedly exercising a restraint on Indian military actions, because Moscow did not

manifest any clear determination to deter China. It was evidently more eager to safeguard its interests and influence both in India and in Pakistan than to side with India.

During the Indo-Pakistan war of 1971 the situation was, however, different. Due to a host of different reasons—including the Indian determination to force Moscow's hand—Soviet leaders helped and sided with India, concluded with her a treaty of co-operation and friendship, warned other nations to remain out of the conflict, and further strengthened their naval power in the Indian Ocean by moving some additional ships into the area. The Chinese made myriad declarations attacking India's policy of dismembering Pakistan—considered vital to China's security—but their capacity of restraining India was severely curtailed by the Soviet presence and the apparent Soviet determination to constrain China not to stymie the Indian objective of partitioning Pakistan.

Thus in this embattled triangle the balance has decisively shifted in favour of Moscow, and China's leverage in the area appears to have been severely curtailed.

For how long such a state of affairs would continue, obviously remains an open question. However, considering the changing nature of alliances in the international system, this may be indeed a temporary Soviet gain that may be changed in the future by other forces and other nations.

Select Bibliography

I. SOURCES

1. Official and Unofficial Publications

CHINA

Ambekar, G.N. and Divekar, V.D. (ed.), *Documents on China's Relations with South and Southeast Asia.* Bombay : 1964.

Foreign Languages Press, *Documents on the Sino-Indian Boundary Question.* Peking : 1960.

——, *The Sino-Indian Boundary Question.* Peking : 1962.

——, *The Polemic on the General Line of the International Communist Movement.* Peking : 1965.

INDIA

Lok Sabha Secretariat, *Foreign Policy of India. Texts of Documents.* New Delhi : 1958.

Ministry of External Affairs, *Prime Minister on Sino-Indian Relations.* 2 Vols. New Delhi : 1962.

——, *Notes, Memoranda, Letters and Agreements between the Governments of India and China 1954-1962.* 6 Vols. New Delhi : 1962.

Ministry of Information and Broadcasting, *Jawaharlal Nehru's Speeches.* 3 Vols. New Delhi : 1958.

PAKISTAN

Harvard University Press, Pakistan. *The Heart of Asia. Speeches by Liaquat Ali Khan.* Cambridge, Mass. : 1950.

Hasan, Sarwar K. (ed.), *Documents on the Foreign Relations of Pakistan : China, India, Pakistan.* Karachi : 1966.

SOVIET UNION

Chernenko, K.U. *et al.* (ed.), *Soviet Foreign Policy. Basic Acts and Documents of the Supreme Soviet of the USSR 1956-62.* Moscow : 1962.

Khruschev, N.S., Soviet Union : *Faithful Friend of the Peoples of the East. N.S. Khruschev's Speeches made during his Visit to India, Burma, Indonesia and Afghanistan.* Moscow : n.d.

— —, *World Without Arms.* 2 Vols. Moscow : n.d.

Lenin, V.I., *The National Liberation Movement in the East.* Moscow : 1957.

— —, *On the Foreign Policy of the Soviet State.* Moscow : n.d.

2. Memoirs, Autobiographies and Journals

Acheson, Dean, *Present at the Creation. My Years in the State Department.* New York : Norton and Company, 1969.

Ayub Khan, Mohammad, *Friends not Masters. A Political Autobiography.* London : Oxford University Press, 1967.

Bowles, Chester, *Ambassador's Report.* New York : Harpers and Brothers, 1954.

Eden, A., *The Reckoning.* London : Cassell, 1965.

Galbraith, John Kenneth, *Ambassador's Journal. A Personal Account of the Kennedy Years.* New York : A Signet Book, 1969.

Khruschev, N.S., *Khruschev Remembers.* New York : Bantam Books, Inc., 1971. (With an introduction, commentary and notes by Edward Crankshaw.)

Menon, K.P.S., *The Flying Troika. Extracts from a Diary.* London : Oxford University Press, 1963.

Nehru, Jawaharlal, *Towards Freedom : The Autobiography of Jawaharlal Nehru.* New York : John Day, 1942.

Pannikar, K.M., *In Two Chinas. Memoirs of a Diplomat.* London : Allen and Unwin, 1955.

Roy, M.N., *M.N. Roy's Memoirs.* Bombay : Allied Publishers Private Ltd., 1964.

3. Newspapers and Periodicals

International Affairs (Moscow)
New China News Agency (Peking)
New Times (Moscow)
Peking Review (Peking)
Pravda (Moscow)
Soviet News (London)

II. STUDIES

1. Books

Bennigsen, Alexandre and Quelquejay, Chantal, *Les mouve-ments nationaux chez les musulmans*. Paris : Mouton, 1960.

Brezizinski, Z. (ed.), *Africa and the Communist World*. Stanford : Stanford University Press, 1963.

Carr, E.H., *The Bolshevik Revolution 1917-1923*, Vol. 3. London : Macmillan, 1953.

Cooley, John K., *East Wind over Africa. Red China's African Offensive*. New York : Walker, 1968.

Deutscher, I., *The Prophet Armed. Trotsky 1879-1921*. London : Oxford University Press, 1954.

Dommen, Arthur J., *Conflict in Laos. The Politics of Neutralization*. London : Pall Mall Press, 1964.

Dutt, Vidya Prakash, *China's Foreign Policy 1958-1962*. New York : Asia Publishing House, 1964.

Eckstein, Alexander, *Communist China's Economic Growth and Trade*. New York : McGraw-Hill Book Company, 1966.

Fifield, Russel H., *The Diplomacy of Southeast Asia 1945-58*. New York : Harper, 1958.

Fitzgerald, C.P., *The Third China*. Vancouver : University of British Columbia, 1965.

Gopal, Ram, *India-China-Tibet Triangle*. Bombay : Jaico Publishing House, 1964.

Greene, Fred, *U.S. Policy and the Security of Asia*. New York : McGraw-Hill Book Company, 1968.

Harick, Arthur, *The Security of China*. London : Chatto and Windus, 1970.

Jain, Girilal, *Panchsheela and After*. Bombay : Asia Publishing House, 1960.

Johnson, Cecil, *Communist China and Latin America 1959-1967*. New York : Columbia University Press, 1970.

Johnstone, William C., *Burma's Foreign Policy*. Cambridge, Mass. : Harvard University Press, 1963.

Kapur, Harish, *Soviet Russia and Asia 1917-27*. London : Michael Joseph, 1966.

——, *The Soviet Union and the Emerging Nations*. London : Michael Joseph, 1971.

Karunakaran, K.P., *India in World Affairs*. 2 Vols. London : Oxford University Press, 1952 and 1958.

Kavic, Lorne J., *India's Quest for Security Defence Policies 1947-1965*. Berkeley : University of California Press, 1967.

Kuusinen, O.V. *et al.*, *Fundamentals of Marxism-Leninism*. Moscow : Foreign Languages Publishing House, 1963.

Leifer, Michael, *Cambodia, the Search for Security*. London : Pall Mall Press, 1968.

Leng, Shao Chuan, *Japan and Communist China*. Kyoto : Doshisha University Press, n.d.

Maxwell, Neville, *India's China War*. London : Jonathan Cape, 1970.

Martens, Pierre and Smets, Paul F., *L'Afrique de Pekin*. Brussels : P. Martens and P. Smets, 1966.

Menon, K.P.S., *China Past and Present*. Bombay : Asia Publishing House, 1968.

Nayar, Kuldip, *Between the Lines*. New Delhi : Allied Publishers Private Ltd., 1969.

Overstreet, Gene D. and Windmiller, Marshall, *Communism in India*. Berkeley : University of California Press, 1959.

Pannikar, K.M., *India and China. A Story of Cultural Relations*. Bombay : Asia Publishing House, 1957.

Passin, Herbert, *China's Cultural Diplomacy*. London : The China Quarterly, 1962.

Poppino, E., *International Communism in Latin America. A History of the Movement 1917-1963*. London : The

Free Press of Glencoe, 1964.

Qureshi, I.H. (ed.), *Foreign Policy of Pakistan, An Analysis*. Karachi : The Allies Book Corporation, 1964.

Richer, Philippe, *La Chine et le tiers monde*.   Paris : Payot, 1971.

Rymalov, V., *La collaboration economique de l'URSS avec les pays sous-developpes*. Moscow : Foreign Languages Press, n.d.

Salisbury, Harrison [E., *Orbit of China*. London : Secker and Worburg, 1967.

Sharma, B.L., *The Pakistan-China Axis*. Bombay : Asia Publishing House, 1967.

Snow, Edgar, *Red China Today*. New York : Random House, 1970.

Spector, Ivor, *The Soviet Union and the Muslim World 1917-1958*. Seattle : University of Washington Press, 1959.

Tang Tsou (ed.), *China's Policies in Asia and America's Alternatives*. Chicago : The University of Chicago Press, 1968.

Troger, Frank N., *Burma from Kingdom to Republic*. London : Pall Mall Press, 1966.

Varma, S.P., *Struggle for the Himalayas*. *A Study in Sino-Indian Relations*. New Delhi : University Publishers, 1965.

Youlou, Fulbert, *J'accuse la Chine*. Paris : La Table Ronde, 1966.

Zagoria, Donald, *Sino-Soviet Conflict 1956-1961*. New York : Atheneum, 1966.

2. Articles

Adie, W.A.C., "China, Russia and the Third World", *The China Quarterly*, July-September 1962.

Gupta, Bhabani Sen, "Moscow, Peking and the Indian Political Scene after Nehru", *Orbis*, Summer 1965.

Kapur, Harish, "India and the Soviet Union", *Survey*, Winter 1971.

Moseley, Philip E., "Soviet Policy in the Developing Countries", *Foreign Affairs*, October 1964.

Nair, K., "Where India, China, Russia Meet", *Foreign Affairs*, January 1958.

Okenberg, Michel, "The Strategies of Peking", *Foreign Affairs*, October 1971.

Ra'anan, Uri, "Moscow and the Third World", *Problems of Communism*, January-February 1965.

Stolte, Stefan C., "The Soviet Union, Communist China and the Underdeveloped Countries", *Institute for the Study of the USSR, Bulletin*, August 1960.

Thornton, Thomas, "Peking, Moscow and the Under-developed Areas", *World Politics*, July 1961.

Ulyanovsky, R., "The Third World"—Problems of Socialist Orientation", *International Affairs*, No. 9, 1971.

3. Newspapers and Journals

Asian Survey (Berkeley)
Economic and Political Weekly (Bombay)
Foreign Affairs (New York)
Foreign Affairs Reports (New Delhi)
India Record (London)
International Herald Tribune (Paris)
Le Monde (Paris)
Link (New Delhi)
Mizan (London)
The China Quarterly (London)
The Statesman's Weekly (Calcutta)

Index